Public Reporting
by Conglomerates

**The Issues, the Problems,
and Some Possible Solutions**

Public Reporting by Conglomerates

The Issues, the Problems, and Some Possible Solutions

Alfred Rappaport
Associate Professor of Accounting
Graduate School of Business Administration
Northwestern University

Peter A. Firmin
W. R. Irby Professor of Accounting
Graduate School of Business Administration
Tulane University

Stephen A. Zeff
Professor of Accounting
Graduate School of Business Administration
Tulane University

PRENTICE-HALL, INC., *Englewood Cliffs, New Jersey*

PRENTICE-HALL INTERNATIONAL, INC., *London*
PRENTICE-HALL OF AUSTRALIA, PTY. LTD., *Sydney*
PRENTICE-HALL OF CANADA, LTD., *Toronto*
PRENTICE-HALL OF INDIA PRIVATE LTD., *New Delhi*
PRENTICE-HALL OF JAPAN, INC., *Tokyo*

Foreword

Call it debate, discussion, or dialogue, Americans seem to be more convinced than ever that talking before acting makes sense. Information is spread, biases revealed, opponents tested, and alliances formed. Hopefully, wiser action follows.

This was the spirit in which a group of people assembled at Tulane University on November 13–14, 1967, to discuss the pros and cons of a controversial issue—public reporting of segmented profit information by corporations in the United States. The Securities and Exchange Commission earlier had made known its intent to require in the near future that corporations report their profits on a segmented basis. Responses by corporate, academic, and accounting spokesmen had been mixed. Some were indifferent, saying that they had been following such a practice for years. Others said that they would not be unhappy to comply, provided that regulations were constructed or construed in some particular way. Others vigorously opposed the idea on conceptual, pragmatic, and emotional grounds. The press and the podium had become the media for discussion, giving the participants little chance to exchange their many views.

Witnessing the debate, Professor Rappaport, formerly of the Tulane Graduate School of Business Administration and now with Northwestern University, Graduate School of Business Administration, conceived the idea of organizing a symposium on this subject. It was his idea that government officials, corporation officers, certified public accountants, stock exchange officers, security analysts, and professors interested and involved in the controversy gather around a conference table for a day and a half.

Testimony to the need and value of such a symposium came quickly when financial sponsors for the Conference were approached. Principal sponsors were Kaiser Industries Corporation, Southern Bell Telephone and Telegraph Company, and Tenneco, Inc., who contributed large sums. Associate sponsors were Arthur Young & Company, General Telephone & Electronics Corporation, and Lockheed Aircraft Corporation. In addition, several sponsors preferred for various reasons to remain anonymous.

In the following pages are presented the papers and a synthesis of

v

the discussions given at the Symposium. Not presented are the many frank, spirited, and thoughtful interactions that took place in the ensuing conversations. Some individuals obtained new insights, some positions were modified, and difficulties and disagreements were made clear. The Symposium, as a prologue to action, was a success.

The Tulane Graduate School of Business Administration was pleased to have been able to host such a Conference, but could not have done so without the much appreciated help of the sponsors. To this must be added a strong vote of appreciation to Professor Rappaport who originated the idea, and to his colleagues, Professors Firmin and Zeff, who assisted him in the organization of the Conference and in the editing of these proceedings.

C. JACKSON GRAYSON, JR.
Dean, Graduate School
of Business Administration
Tulane University

Preface

Corporate growth through combination of diverse and often unrelated activities, services, or products—often in widely separated geographical regions of the world—is one of the intriguing phenomena of our time. Corporations which carry on such operations are termed "conglomerates."

Investors, security analysts, certain agencies in the United States government, and other external parties interested in corporate operations have complained that particularly in the case of conglomerate organizations, information which is relevant if not vital to rational investment decision-making is not provided by traditional methods of corporate financial reporting. To be useful, it is argued, financial reports must facilitate evaluation of operations by some corporate segment such as market served, industry classification, product-line grouping, or internal corporate structure.

Opponents of this contention charge that the conglomerate organization must be viewed as a total system and that segmental reporting of the operations of such corporations will not necessarily enhance the ability of external parties to evaluate operations or to make rational investment decisions.

To discuss these views in an uninhibited way, Tulane University provided a symposium, the proceedings of which are reported here, in hopes that through such discussion reasonable and socially desirable solutions might be obtained.

Efforts such as this one owe their success to the cooperative effort of many people. We take this opportunity to thank the sponsors and associate sponsors (listed elsewhere in this document) who provided the Graduate School of Business Administration at Tulane University with the financial resources necessary to conduct this symposium. Special acknowledgement is made of the contribution of Dean C. Jackson Grayson, Jr. of the Graduate School of Business Administration at Tulane University, who assisted in the planning phases of the symposium and who served as discussion leader in one segment of the program. The contribution of A. A. Sommer, Jr. who provided the background paper for the symposium is also explicitly acknowledged. The special role of Streuby L. Drumm, who provided valuable counsel and delivered the official welcome, is noted. The contributions of Mrs. Doris Campbell and Mrs. Ann Hopkins, who provided the administrative and secretarial assistance so necessary to programs such as these, deserve special mention. And finally, to all of the participants who gave so generously of their time and energy by accepting our invitations to come to New Orleans to discuss the central issue, we acknowledge our debt of thanks.

ALFRED RAPPAPORT
PETER A. FIRMIN
STEPHEN A. ZEFF

New Orleans, Louisiana

Sponsors

Speakers

A. A. SOMMER, JR.

B.A., University of Notre Dame; LL.B., Harvard Law School. Partner, Calfee, Halter, Calfee, Griswold & Sommer, Cleveland, Ohio. Member Board of Directors, The Welfare Federation, Ohio State Bar Association, Cleveland Bar Association, American Bar Association. Chairman of the Tax Policy ACTION Committee, and Trustee, Notre Dame Law Association. Has published and lectured on legal aspects of accounting, taxation, and securities.

ANDREW BARR

B.S., M.S., University of Illinois; CPA. Chief Accountant, Securities and Exchange Commission. On accounting faculty at Yale University for twelve years. Has served as president, Federal Government Accountants Association, and National Association of Accountants, Washington Chapter; and as vice president, American Accounting Association.

JOHN M. BLAIR

B.A., Tulane University; Ph.D., American University, Washington, D.C. Chief Economist, Senate Antitrust and Monopoly Subcommittee. Served on Temporary National Economic Committee, 1939–41, and War Production Board, 1942–43. Was Chief Economist, Smaller War Plants Commission, and Assistant Chief Economist, Federal Trade Commission. Has lectured and contributed papers in the fields of industrial organization, pricing policy, technical change, economic concentration, and monopolistic policies.

DUDLEY E. BROWNE

B.A., University of California at Los Angeles; CPA. Group Vice President—Finance and Administration, Lockheed Aircraft Corporation, Burbank, California. A director of Lockheed Aircraft International, Inc. and Lockheed Air Terminal, Inc. Past President, Financial Executives Institute and Financial Executives Research Foundation. Was Hoover Commission task force member on budget and accounting. Chairman of UCLA Foundation and member of numerous civic boards dealing with financial matters.

W. DAVID MACCALLAN

B.Sc., M.A., McGill University, Montreal, P.Q.; CFA. Security analyst, Adams Express Company, New York, New York, having served as Assistant Vice President and Vice President—Research. Formerly security analyst with Sun Life Assurance Company of Canada and Bank of New York.

ROBERT E. PFENNING

B.S., Lafayette College. Comptroller and a member of the Executive Office of General Electric Company. Chairman of pension board, trustee of the General Electric Foundation, General Electric Pension Trust, and several related trusts. A director of the Financial Executives Institute.

JOHN HARTMANN

B.S., University of Santa Clara; M.B.A., Stanford University; CPA. Vice President, Finance and Planning, Kern County Land Company, San Francisco, California. Member Executive Committee, Council of California Growers, member Board of Directors, J. I. Case Company and Watkins-Johnson Company; president, Stanford Business School Association; on advisory board, School of Business Administration, University of Santa Clara.

C. REED PARKER

B.A., M.B.A., Dartmouth College; LL.B., Chicago-Kent College of Law; CFA. Vice President, Duff, Anderson & Clark, Inc., Chicago, Illinois. President of Investment Analysts Society of Chicago. Associate Editor, *Financial Analysts Journal*; chairman of the Board of Regents of the Financial Analysts Seminar.

NEWMAN T. HALVORSON

B.A., University of Wisconsin; CPA. Partner, Ernst & Ernst, national office, Cleveland, Ohio. Member of the Accounting Principles Board of the AICPA.

Presently on subcommittee of the APB acting as liaison between APB and the Financial Executives Institute committee directing the FEI research project on reporting by conglomerates. Past member, AICPA Committees on Accounting Procedure, Auditing Procedure, and Relations with the SEC and Stock Exchanges.

SIDNEY DAVIDSON

Ph.D., University of Michigan; CPA. Arthur Young Professor of Accounting and Director of the Institute of Professional Accounting in the Graduate School of Business, University of Chicago. Was Professor of Accounting at the Johns Hopkins University. Has taught at the Universities of California, Hawaii, Michigan, Stanford, and the London School of Economics. Member of the Accounting Principles Board of the AICPA. 1968–69 president-elect of the American Accounting Association. Consultant to the U. S. Treasury Department on taxation matters.

DAVID SOLOMONS

B.Com., D.Sc., London School of Economics. Professor of Accounting, Wharton School of Finance and Commerce, University of Pennsylvania. Fellow of the Institute of Chartered Accountants in England and Wales. Has taught at London School of Economics, IMEDE (Management Development Institute) in Switzerland, and at the Universities of London, Bristol, California (Berkeley), and Auckland, New Zealand. Member of professional organizations in economics, management sciences and accounting in England and the United States. Has engaged in research on international business, and has published in the fields of managerial economics, financial management, and accounting.

MICHAEL N. CHETKOVICH

B.S., M.S., University of California (Berkeley); CPA. Partner, Haskins & Sells, executive office, New York, New York. Member of American Institute of CPA's, California Society of CPA's, American Accounting Association, and Institute of Internal Auditors.

Contents

Public Reporting
by Conglomerates

**The Issues, the Problems,
and Some Possible Solutions**

A. A. SOMMER, JR.*

Conglomerate Disclosure:

Friend or Foe?

*J. of accountancy
may 1947 pv1-u7*

The life of the accountant has perhaps never been an easy one; his life today has perhaps never been more difficult. In addition to the more routine kinds of pressure to which he is subjected by the rigors of deadlines and the insistences of clients, there have been added recently increased hazards of litigation (more than eighty suits were pending in March, 1966 naming accountants as defendants [1] and the figure is now probably more than a hundred), the impatience of the Securities and Exchange Commission with the slowness of accounting organizations in resolving problems,[2] the heightened insistence for reform in the direction of establishing a single set of accounting principles.[3] It is no exaggeration to suggest that the accounting profession is experiencing its most trying period since the McKesson & Robbins episode of three decades ago.

Added to the other problems confronting the accounting profession —and the financial and industrial community as well—is the recently highlighted problem of appropriate financial reporting for the "conglomerate" enterprise.

In response to many forces in American economic life, including the increasing hostility of courts and administrative agencies to horizontal and vertical acquisitions by all save the possessors of very small fragments of a market,[4] aggressive managements have turned increasingly to the con-

---

* This is a revised and updated version of Mr. Sommer's earlier paper appearing in the January, 1967 issue of *The Business Lawyer*. We wish to thank the editors of *The Business Lawyer* for their permission to publish this paper.

[1] *New York Times*, March 27, 1966.

[2] This found expression in the Commission's Acounting Series Release No. 102, *Balance Sheet Classification of Deferred Income Taxes Arising From Installment Sales*.

[3] Address by Manuel F. Cohen before the Seventy-Ninth Annual Meeting of the American Institute of Certified Public Accountants, page 4, reprinted in *The Journal of Accountancy*, December, 1966, p. 58.

[4] In United States v. Von's Grocery Co., 384 U. S. 270 (1966) the court declared that the acquisition by a competitor with 4.7% of sales in the relevant area of a company with 4.2% of sales in the area constituted a violation of Section 7 of the Clayton Act.

glomerate "merger" as the means of growth through acquisition. The remoteness of the activity of the acquired enterprise from the previous range of activities of the acquiring company may range from the relationship of a shipbuilding firm to a company making, among other things, typewriters and business machines, to the simple acquisition of a company manufacturing a low-priced version of a higher-priced product manufactured by the acquiring company.

These so-called "conglomerate" or perhaps more gracefully, "diversification," acquisitions have increasingly been the subject matter of attack by the Anti-Trust Division of the Department of Justice and the Federal Trade Commission.[5] The Supreme Court has recently determined that a conglomerate merger may violate Section 7 of the Clayton Act, although there is considerable question as to how broadly this opinion can be applied.[6]

Such acquisitions have also become the subject of attention from Congress. During the early part of 1965 the Subcommittee on Anti-Trust and Monopoly of the Senate Committee on the Judiciary headed by Senator Philip A. Hart of Michigan held hearings on "Mergers and Other Factors Affecting Industry Concentration." During the course of these hearings the subcommittee heard considerable testimony concerning the effects of conglomerate acquisitions on the American economy. Among others Professor Joel Dirlam of Rhode Island University stressed the absence of factual information from which appropriate conclusions might be drawn concerning the effects of such acquisitions. He said:

> The relative profitability of different divisions and product lines should be brought out in order to appraise the competitive tactics utilizing diversification. We are operating in almost complete ignorance in this area when we do not know even the sales of many of the major firms in different lines, let alone the profitability or losses incurred in these lines. We cannot reach a judgment which is supportable in proposing legislation or changes in public policy. I would speak also on behalf of the average investor who does not know what he is buying into when he purchases one of these large diversified firms. He has only the overall statement to go by. He judges then not the industry but the behavior of the firm itself, and he stakes his money on the management with a minimum of information. . . . On a more limited scale, I do not think that an amendment to the Securities and Exchange Act [sic] could require that corporations disclose on a fuller basis than they do now their sales and operating income from different activities in which they may be engaged. Such knowledge should be available both to the average investor and the antitrust authorities.[7]

Professor Dirlam ventured further into the securities area by relating the opinion of a Wall Street friend who expressed the thought that there

[5] Bock, *Mergers and Markets* (5th Edition, 1966) pp. 140–191.
[6] F. T. C. v. Procter & Gamble Co., 386 W.S. 568 (1967).
[7] Hearings before the Subcommittee on Anti-Trust and Monopoly, Committee on the Judiciary, United States Senate, Eighty-Ninth Congress, First Session, p. 769.

was insufficient information about such enterprises from which to make adequate investment judgments.

Senator Hart understandably followed through on the testimony of Professor Dirlam by asking Chairman Manuel F. Cohen of the Securities and Exchange Commission for the Commission's reaction to his suggestions for augmented reporting. Chairman Cohen responded with a detailed staff memorandum expressing the extent to which present reporting procedures and forms require product-line and similar partial activity reporting.[8] The memorandum concluded with the assertion that in the Commission's estimation it presently had the power to compel additional detailed disclosure, including that recommended by Professor Dirlam, but had "refrained from seeking disclosure of information regarding each product or service in terms of operating or net income" because of a variety of considerations detailed in the memorandum including, not insignificantly, many of those now being thrust at the Commission by the foes of divisional reporting. Reading the memorandum the conclusion of one publication that the initial response of the Commission was "cautious" was indeed justified.[9]

The attitude of the Commission has changed. Relative unconcern has been supplanted by frequent repetitions of concern and urgings of haste by industry and professional groups in giving the Commission the benefit of their thoughts on the problem. The subject received extended attention in the speeches of Mr. Cohen before the Annual Conference of the Financial Analysts Federation and the Annual Meeting of the American Institute of Certified Public Accountants, and was the content of his testimony before Senator Hart's Subcommittee in September, 1966.

As a consequence of this rising tempo of official concern interested groups have quickly moved into intensive activity. The American Institute of Certified Public Accountants constituted its Committee on Relations with Securities and Exchange Commission and Stock Exchanges an ad hoc committee to look initially at the matter and furnished to the Commission a comprehensive 12-page discussion of the problem and the role of accountants in solving it.

More recently, in September, 1967 the Accounting Principles Board in a statement (*not* an opinion) discussed the problem and indicated that before it could make a "definitive" pronouncement considerable research was necessary with respect to the need of investors for conglomerate disclosure, the reliability of such disclosure for investment decisions, the extent to which such disclosure might be harmful to the reporting company, and the extent to which such disclosure was necessary for a fair presentation of financial position and results of operations. Meanwhile it urged corporations to renew their disclosure practices with an eye to their possible expansion.

The Financial Executives Institute through its foundation has almost

[8] Id. at pp. 1069–1071.
[9] *Forbes,* July 15, 1966, pp. 16–7.

completed a comprehensive study under the direction of Professor Robert K. Mautz of the University of Illinois which will undoubtedly be most influential in charting the direction of future conglomerate disclosure practices. Professor Mautz has organized his study on two levels: conceptual and pragmatic. The conceptual portion has consisted of three papers published in *The Financial Executive* (July, September, and November, 1967) discussing the characteristics of the "conglomerate," the extent to which the reliability of conglomerate disclosures may be diminished by intra-corporation sales and central cost allocations, and the various methods of dividing or segmenting the enterprise. On the pragmatic level, questionnaires were sent to virtually all of the major corporate enterprises in the United States (as well as many smaller ones) asking information concerning their internal segmental reporting practices and their thoughts as to how such internal practices could lend themselves to external reporting. In addition, questionnaires were circulated among financial analysts in an effort to determine their needs. The results of this study are expected in early 1968.

All the while the Commission stands in the wings saying, "Hurry, hurry, hurry."

This brief history tells the story of a problem which originally arose in the context of antitrust but quickly acquired the guise of a disclosure problem. It is only fair to say, however, that others besides those in official positions have raised similar questions. Herman W. Bevis, Senior Partner of Price Waterhouse & Co., has remarked:

> A somewhat different type of reporting problem exists where an enterprise consists of two or more segments in distinctly different lines of business, or under differing geographical influences, or otherwise clearly subject to different trends and risks. Whether such an enterprise is consolidated or not, and even whether it consists of divisions rather than subsidiaries, careful consideration needs to be given to the disclosure of available, pertinent information about each important segment. . . . Some corporations segment their operations by major product lines and disclose the sales volume of each. A very few report in general or specific terms about net incomes of one or more of these lines. *Any information of this type is highly useful to the stockholder. . . . This reporting of meaningful data about major separable segments of the entire enterprise deserves careful consideration by all corporate managements.*[10] (Emphasis added)

Nor is concern with the problem confined to this country. The English Parliament recently adopted the Companies Act 1967, Chapter 81, which contains the new provision (Section 17) quoted in part below:

"If, in the course of a financial year, a company . . . has carried on business of two or more classes . . . that, in the opinion of the directors, differ sub-

[10] Bevis, *Corporate Financial Reporting in a Competitive Economy* (1965) p. 155–6.

stantially from each other, there shall be contained in the director's report relating to that year a statement of—

    a. the proportions in which the turnover [i.e. sales] for that year . . . is divided amongst those classes (describing them); and

    b. as regards business of each class, the extent or approximate extent (expressed, in either case, in monetary terms) to which, in the opinion of the directors, the carrying on of business of that class contributed to, or restricted, the profit or loss of the company for that year before taxation." [11]

Precisely, what is the problem? Basically the problem is not one of disclosing *revenues* from various activity; in most significant situations those must be disclosed now under relevant Commission procedures and rules.

Form S-1, the general form used to register securities under the Securities Act of 1933, and Form 10, the comprehensive form for registering securities under the Securities Exchange Act of 1934, both require that:

If the business consists of the production or distribution of different kinds of products or the rendering of different kinds of services, indicate, insofar as practicable, the relative importance of each product or service or class of similar products or services which contributed 15% or more to the gross volume of business done during the last fiscal year.[12]

Furthermore, the form required to be filed annually by all listed companies and unlisted companies registered under Section 12(g) of the '34 Act (as well as a few others), Form 10-K, contains similar requirements with respect to changes in the business of the reporting enterprise during the year.[13] Also, Form 8-K, which is used to report certain corporate events promptly after their occurrence, requires disclosure of comprehensive financial and other information concerning any acquisition of a "significant" amount of assets, and "significant" for these purposes is defined to mean assets exceeding 15 percent of the registrant's consolidated total assets, or a business whose gross revenue for its last fiscal year exceeded 15 percent of the aggregate gross revenues of the registrant on a consolidated basis (it has been proposed that this percentage be reduced to 10 percent).[14] Further, Rule 5-03 under the Commission's regulation S-X requires that if an issuer derives revenues from both sales and services, and each exceeds 10 percent of the total, the contribution of each to gross income must be disclosed.

The problem, then, is disclosure of the extent to which the several segments of a business contribute to the overall profitability of the entire enterprise, with probable concomitant disclosure of such related matters

[11] The London Stock Exchange has imposed similar requirements with respect to companies whose securities are newly listed on that Exchange. *Accountancy*, April, 1965, p. 300.

[12] Item 9, Form S-1; Item 3, Form 10.

[13] Item 4.

[14] Item 2.

as gross margins, utilization of borrowed capital, overhead charges and the like. And the threshold problem, as Chairman Cohen labelled it, is what constitutes a "division" or "line of products"—i.e., a segment of the business —as to which such separate disclosure shall be made.[15]

To appreciate the nature of the proposed extension of reporting it is desirable to recall quickly the form which financial reporting now conventionally takes. Historically the basic reporting entity is defined by the outer limits of the economic activity in which the investment of the owners of the enterprise is utilized. This may take the form of a proprietorship or a partnership, both of which have net worth accounts that are substantially similar. Most significant economic entities are organized as corporations, and generally, even when there are parent-subsidiary relations and only consolidated statements are published, each corporation is a separate, identifiable entity for preliminary accounting purposes at least. In any event, it is fundamental that "any report on the activity [of a unit or entity] must identify clearly the particular unit or entity involved." [16] And a business entity is defined as ". . . an organization of persons and property which have been brought together for certain economic objectives." [17]

Even when the ultimate report is consolidated it is still a report of the entity in which the shareholders of the parent corporation have their investment at work. It has long been a truism that in many situations only a consolidated statement gives a true presentation of the significant enterprise, and in recognition of this the Securities and Exchange Commission in most instances where there are parents and subsidiaries permits omission of the separate statements of the parent and subsidiaries if appropriate consolidated statements are included.[18] However, consolidating statements will be prepared in the course of preparing consolidated statements even if they are not publicly disclosed. That there are circumstances in which consolidated reporting is inappropriate and segmented reporting is appropriate is evident: for instance, it is generally considered improper accounting procedure to consolidate the accounts of such distinctive operations as those of banking, finance, and insurance subsidiaries with those of an industrial parent, although in some circumstances this is permissible.[19]

[15] Statement of Manuel F. Cohen to the Subcommittee on Anti-Trust and Monopoly, Committee on the Judiciary, United States Senate, September 20, 1966, p. 1986.

[16] Sprouse and Moonitz, *A Tentative Set of Broad Accounting Principles for Business Enterprises*, (1962) p. 6.

[17] Grady, *Inventory of Generally Accepted Acounting Principles for Business Enterprises*, (1965) p. 26.

[18] For instance, Paragraph A.3. of "Instructions as to Financial Statements" constituting part of Form S-1 provides for the omission of the registrant's financial statements if consolidated statements are filed and the registrant is primarily an operating company and all subsidiaries included in the consolidated financial statements are totally-held subsidiaries or the registrant's total assets (exclusive of investments in and advances to consolidated subsidiaries) constitute 85% or more of the total assets shown by the consolidated balance sheet and the registrant's total gross revenues constitute 85% or more of the total gross revenues shown by the consolidated profit and loss statements filed.

[19] Accounting Research Bulletin No. 51, *Consolidated Financial Statements* (1959).

All of this, of course, is predicated upon the assumption that the economic (and accounting) unit corresponds to the legal unit, i.e., the corporation. While

> consolidated statements are the result of an endeavor to cut across legal entities and to present the financial and operating position of the economic unit composed of several legal entities subject to a unified control through stock ownership,[20]

still even in consolidated statements the irreducible building blocks are separate legal entities.

While to some extent conglomerate reporting might in some instances entail little more than disclosure of the consolidating statements of subsidiaries, the demands of those wishing greater reporting are not limited to that; they seek reporting determined in scope less by legal entities and legal relationships and more by economic activities.

The proposal to report the profits of segments of an enterprise, of course, poses a host of questions, most of which are offshoots of these two questions: 1) to what extent is it necessary or desirable that additional disclosure be made, and 2) to what extent can such disclosure be made meaningfully and helpfully? Around these questions most of the discussion has centered, upon these presumably the study of the Financial Executives Institute will focus.

The first question, the necessity or desirability of such reporting, immediately provokes substantial controversy. The investment community—and in this instance at least including many otherwise more commonly found opposing the Commission—finds much to support in the Commission effort. It is their contention, articulated to the Hart subcommittee by Yura Arkus-Duntov, an investment officer with The Dreyfus Corp., managers and underwriters of the Dreyfus Fund, Inc., that without product-line or otherwise sequenced reporting it is impossible for the investor to make an intelligent investment decision with respect to a conglomerate. Mr. Arkus-Duntov cited this example:

> . . . take the case of a $1 billion "conglomerate" company in which after dissecting its operations, one would have found that it had a division having a product distinctly unrelated to the main, historical business of the company and that this division contributed only 5 percent to gross revenues but 30 percent to profits. This imbalance in profits resulted not from the outstanding performance of the particular division but, rather, from the very poor performance of the main business of the company. These facts, however, were not available in published reports and could not have been determined at that time unless one were on the "inside" or had the benefit of

---

[20] Quoted from Kester in the *Accountants' Handbook*, ed. Wixon (4th ed.; New York: The Ronald Press Company, 1956), Sec. 23, p. 1.

"inside" information. An investment in the company, therefore, had to be considered on the basis of wholly inadequate information.[21]

The argument posed against this, of course, is that the investor is investing in the enterprise as a whole, not in the particular segments as such, and that consequently it should not matter to him how any single segment is performing if the overall result is satisfactory. The rejoinder is that product-line reporting may give significant clues to future performance: "We're interested in having as complete information as possible on where companies' profits come from. It's especially helpful in forecasting earnings in the future. If a division that has been losing can break even, it can make a big difference in earnings." [22] Further, the desirability of measuring performance of a segment against the results of the independent competing with the segment is frequently stressed. Also Chairman Cohen has argued:

> It [divisional disclosure] . . . serves as an important control on corporate managers by requiring them to justify the results of their stewardship. There may be diversified companies which are maintaining low-profit or money-losing operations for reasons which would not be persuasive to stockholders or financial analysts, and requiring separate disclosure might well result in the improvement or elimination of the substandard operation, to the ultimate benefit of the stockholders and of the economy generally. Finally, we may well find, as we have in other areas, that a requirement of public disclosure will result in improvements in internal accounting procedures that will provide the company managements themselves with more useful information to evaluate the performance of their various divisions.[23]

As noted, the problem of conglomerate reporting moved to front stage as a consequence of an antitrust inquiry, and it is in this context that the social desirability of requiring such reporting is most emphatically stated. The principal argument in this area is that such disclosure is necessary to permit analysis of the extent of concentration in an industry; for instance, unless Litton Industries and IBM disclose the volume of their typewriter sales, it is difficult to determine the extent of concentration in that industry. Query, however, whether this kind of economic analysis requires that anything more than revenues be disclosed—a disclosure already required to a large extent under present rules and one which avoids most of the complexities of the profit contribution disclosure being urged.

Dr. Willard F. Mueller, director of the Federal Trade Commission's Bureau of Economics, testified that segmented reporting was a necessity for free competition to be effective. He said that such disclosure would indi-

---

[21] Hearings before the Subcommittee on Anti-Trust and Monopoly, Committee on the Judiciary, United States Senate, Eighty-Ninth Congress, First Session, p. 1706.

[22] *Forbes*, July 15, 1966, p. 17, quoting Paul Trevor, vice president of the Affiliated Fund.

[23] Address by Manuel F. Cohen before the Seventy-Ninth Annual Meeting of the American Institute of Certified Public Accountants, p. 7, reprinted in *The Journal of Accountancy*, December 1966, p. 59.

cate to potential competition the desirability of competing in a given market, that it would prevent a conglomerate food enterprise from over-charging in one area to subsidize operations in another area of more intense competition, and that it would preclude improper use of economic power by the conglomerate.[24] It it interesting that Dr. Mueller's conception of appropriate reporting would, at least in the food industry, embrace separate reporting by geographical regions as well as by product-line or other segment.

One of the arguments frequently voiced against requiring such reporting is the adverse competitive impact on the reporting company. In a sense this is the reverse of the argument of the advocates who contend that failure to report segmentally has anti-competitive consequences because it shelters a unit from the competition of those who might enter a market where profit is high. The argument of the opponents asserts that by compelling such disclosure competitors may learn about profitability, margins, cost of sales and the like. To the extent that information about total sales is the bear, it is a myth, since as seen this degree of disclosure is commonly required under existing Commission rules. As for the other information, there is some question concerning the extent to which competitors live in such ignorance,[25] and further, there is some belief that American industry over-reacts to the danger of educating competition. Also it should not be forgotten that many of the competitors of the conglomerates are unsegmented enterprises with a single product line who must now if they are subject to SEC reporting requirements make full public disclosure of these sensitive items. It may reasonably be asked whether absence of segmented reporting does not result in inequitable competitive advantages to the conglomerate who may obscure the same information his competitors must disclose. Perhaps of more consequence than enlightening competitors is the danger of over-educating customers: specialized businesses with a few large customers might find it embarrassing at least, and hazardous to profits at worst, if their customers learned their profit margins.

When the discussion moves into the area of how such disclosures could be made meaningfully and helpfully the difficulty increases. There is first the problem of deciding which companies would have to report on the segmented basis. Litton Industries is perhaps the modern classic of the conglomerate; is General Motors? What of American Telephone and Telegraph with its myriad of geographical subsidiaries? The ad hoc committee of the American Institute of Certified Public Accountants suggested preliminarily these characteristics:

1. It (the enterprise) became a "conglomerate" by the acquisition of businesses operating in widely divergent industries.

[24] Statement of Dr. Willard F. Mueller before the Subcommittee on Anti-Trust and Monopoly, Committee on the Judiciary, United States Senate, September 12, 1966, p. 1864 ff.
[25] Forbes, July 15, 1966, p. 17.

2. It operates the acquired businesses on a highly decentralized basis, with decentralized management and accounting information.

3. It has few common manufacturing or distribution facilities, and rarely engages in transferring products between divisions.

4. It has a limited amount of "joint costs" except for financing and central administration.[26]

The committee recognized that some enterprises which begin as conglomerates would in time lose their conformity to the guides and become integrated, thus terminating the necessity—or at least the feasibility—of continued separate reporting.

The Committee's approach would exclude from conglomerate reporting requirements the enterprise which had achieved the external characteristics of a conglomerate—participation in widely varying industries, for example—by internal growth and expansion. And of course it would exclude the enterprise which by acquisition or internal growth had expanded vertically or horizontally.

Dr. Mueller has proposed different, and much broader, standards. Conglomerate enterprises according to him are

1. . . . much larger, in the absolute sense, than their competitors;

2. they operate across a larger number of separate economic markets;

3. they occupy much larger market positions in some markets than in others;

4. (they) meet one another with increasing frequency in their respective markets.[27]

Next of course, there is the problem of identifying the segments with respect to which separate reporting should be done. If American industry were organized with each product line neatly sheltered in a separate subsidiary, there would be no problem: simply report the operating results of each subsidiary. But, of course, no such neat pattern of corporate organization exists; one conglomerate may operate through the medium of subsidiaries separately organized, another through divisions.

Should the reporting be by divisions (regardless of how the particular enterprise has organized them), product line, geographical area, functional activity (manufacturing, wholesaling, retailing)? If by divisions as established by the enterprise itself, one of the benefits which would supposedly accrue from such reporting would be lost—comparability of results, since divisionalization is far from uniform. Not uncommonly groups of activity are brought under a divisional shelter for reasons unique to the enterprise.

[26] Letter, Committee on Relations with Securities and Exchange Commission and Stock Exchanges to Clifford V. Heimbucher, September 2, 1966.
[27] Statement of Dr. Willard F. Mueller before the Subcommittee on Anti-Trust and Monopoly, Committee on the Judiciary, United States Senate, September 12, 1966, p. 1865.

The difficulties of using divisions are highlighted by the testimony of Mr. George M. Bunker, President of Martin Marietta Company, Inc., who appeared as something of a hero before the Hart subcommittee because of the recently adopted practice of Martin Marietta in reporting profits divisionally. Mr. Bunker stated that one of the separately reporting divisions was Martin Marietta's Chemical Division which he said included "printing ink, dyestuffs, concrete additives and the industrial sand businesses." [28] Compare this "chemical division" with the "chemicals group" of The Glidden Company which includes titanium dioxide, copper, tin, lead and other ferrous and non-ferrous powders, basic and fine terpine products, as well as a number of other products.

Product-line reporting is no easy solution, either. There is, of course, the problem of defining the product lines; for instance, does General Motors have five passenger automobile product lines or a single product line consisting of passenger automobiles? Reverting to the comparison of Martin Marietta and Glidden in the chemical field, what are the pertinent product lines? As for geographical breakdowns, the instances in which these would be conceivably pertinent are, of course, relatively few, e.g., the national grocery chains discussed by Dr. Mueller, and hence would be of little use in resolving the dilemma of how to segment the reporting corporate complex.

Of course, the complexity of this part of the problem runs from simple to the near impossible. Some conglomerates—those most characteristically so in terms of the definition suggested by the American Institute of Certified Public Accountants above—are relatively easy: their operations are neatly sorted out into subsidiaries or easily identified divisions. Yet even in those instances there may be aberrations within the subsidiaries or divisions that reduce the value of comparing them with independent units *generally* in the same business but not precisely so. At the other end of the spectrum is the diversified company with large groupings and intricate intertwinings that virtually defy meaningful classification of lines. If segmented reporting is to perform its role significantly some means of delineation will have to be developed which will be applicable to at least a large part of this spectrum.

Even if one gets past this hurdle, the next problem is how significant a part of the entire enterprises' business should the segment be to require separate reporting? For instance, if 10 percent is the norm, then a product line with sales of a million dollars would have to be reported by a conglomerate with nine million dollars of sales, but not by any conglomerate with more than ten million dollars of sales; again comparability suffers. If the criterion were in the alternative of gross dollars or percentages, the largest corporations fitting in the category of conglomerate would of neces-

---

[28] Testimony of George M. Bunker before the Subcommittee on Anti-Trust and Monopoly, Committee on the Judiciary, United States Senate, p. 1973.

sity bury the public in a myriad of statistics and thus defeat the worth of the undertaking.

It would appear that in any event, regardless of the method of identifying segments used, rarely will they be neatly carved off from the whole, and this circumstance of course will require considerable explanation of wherein the incision was less than precise, and this too will minimize the value of the newly disclosed information.

Once the conglomerate is identified and practicable standards for dividing it into reporting segments are established, there remains the complex problem of determining what should be reported. It is commonplace in any large enterprise that for management purposes there is internal divisional or product-line reporting, if for no other reason than to permit intelligent judgment of the performance of line management. However, the methods by which the profit performance is ascertained and their limitations are realized and understood by those reviewing, and there is no reliance placed upon the information other than to judge divisional performance. Yet even this has complexities which have merited extensive treatment in a 1965 publication of the Financial Executives Institute, *Divisional Performance: Measurement and Control,* by David Solomons.

But preparation and use of such figures for these purposes is a far cry from their preparation and use for public disclosure.

The principal problem is one of allocations. Assuming the simplest case, that the product with respect to which reporting is required is produced in a single plant which produces no other product and the entire production is sold through an independent marketing organization, there are obviously many allocations which would be required for full comprehension of the profitability of the segment. If the corporation has borrowed capital or preferred stock, what assumptions should be made in connection with the use of that capital as opposed to the capital represented by common stock? Make the problem a little more intricate: suppose the plant and working capital of the segment are financed entirely out of the proceeds of a public offering of debt? Should the entire cost of the funds raised be charged to the one activity?

Another problem is that of allocating central office overhead and research and development. In any given year central office expenses and resarch and development costs may relate to a particular product line in vast disproportion to any common measure which might be used—sales, use of capital, total investment, and so on. Shouldn't an adequate system of profit reporting make provision for these peculiarities, for surely they would be reflected in the profit results of a single product corporation?

There are also the myriad problems of allocating the expenses of institutional advertising, income taxes, charitable contributions. Even so simple an item as gross sales may become a demon of complexity if a reporting segment makes intra-corporate sales.

The Commission in its memorandum to Senator Hart elaborated a further hazard in the area of allocation. The staff gave this example:

> For example, in a given consolidated group of companies a single product line might be produced by several subsidiary companies, each of which also produces several other products, while the parent company absorbs all research and development costs. . . .[29]

The lot of the conglomerate would not be easy under almost any system of segmented reporting.

An example of the distortions which can result when a portion of overall corporate activity is reported is contained in the letter of the American Institute of Certified Public Accountants committee which considered this problem:

> Many companies have reported overseas "profits" and analysts have compared these profits with U. S. profits and may have drawn misleading conclusions. The reason is that U. S. costs frequently include the overall costs of research, product and manpower development and marketing techniques. Overseas operations frequently benefit from the U. S. costs. Only those products are marketed overseas which have been refined and developed in the U. S. Thus the reported overseas "profits" tend to be "incremental" profits and are dependent upon the U. S. activity. Comparable U. S. profits would require the elimination of all the "joint costs" charged to U. S. operations.[30]

Even if some method of allocation can be developed, there is the danger that the results of such allocation may be grossly misunderstood. For instance, assume that General Electric was compelled to disclose separately the performance of its nuclear power division. For years this would have shown substantial red ink, a circumstance that would inevitably have raised questions in the eyes of some investors and analysts as to the desirability of subsidizing this development with the profits of other operations. May not one consequence of requiring segmented disclosure be a dampening of the enthusiasm of management for engaging in developmental activity if its cost may have to be separately disclosed, particularly when such costs may never result in a profitable operation—giving rise, in a climate increasingly hospitable to the suing shareholder, to possible charges of mismanagement? The question may well be asked whether it may not be socially desirable to permit the management of conglomerates to shield developmental expense behind the corporate veil.

The suggestion has been made that the final expression of the profitability of a segment of the enterprise be a "defined profit" instead of the

---

[29] Hearings before the Subcommittee on Anti-Trust and Monopoly, Committee on the Judiciary, United States Senate, Eighty-Ninth Congress, First Session, p. 1071.

[30] Letter, Committee on Relations with Securities and Exchange Commission and Stock Exchanges to Clifford V. Heimbucher, September 2, 1966.

conventional profit figure. The "defined profit" would exclude virtually all of the allocable costs and confine the profit computation to those items which pertain clearly to the product line or segment, thus side-stepping all of the complexities of allocation. It has been suggested that this could readily give rise to exaggerated or misleading notions of profitability in many quarters—competitors, unions, would-be competitors, and would only introduce a new and unwelcome element of uncertainty. It may certainly be said that it would destroy much of the comparability of performance as between a conglomerate division and its competing single-product enterprise. Furthermore if the desire is to make meaningful disclosure to investors, it surely falls short of that when important elements that help determine profitability are excluded.

A facet of the problem which appears to have been but little discussed (except by Mr. Louis H. Rappaport and a few others) is the segmented balance sheet. If segmented reporting is to be of assistance to the investment analyst and the investor certainly one of the most important bits of information will be return on investment; this is perhaps the single most valuable measure of management performance. To calculate this ratio it is necessary obviously to determine the investment in the division; to do this there must be prepared a segmented balance sheet; and this balance sheet should properly reflect *all* of the assets used by the segment and *all* of its liabilities, else the investment on which the return is calculated will be plainly erroneous and the ratio misleading.

The preparation of such a balance sheet involves allocation problems even more perplexing than the problems of allocating for purposes of the income statement. How shall a corporation's investment in a laboratory used for several lines of research be allocated? How shall the central office building be allocated? How shall the company airplane be allocated? There recurs again the problem of dealing with borrowed capital and allocating its amount as well as its cost. A case can be made perhaps for using sales, use, or some such measure as a crude means of allocating expenses. It is apparent, however, that to use such fluctuating norms in making balance sheet allocations will result in balance sheet adjustments of a kind completely at variance with those conventionally allowed. And yet, despite the patent difficulties, if segmented reporting is to achieve its goal of helping the investor this series of obstacles will have to be confronted and overcome.

Frequently cited in support of the feasibility of divisional reporting are a handful of major conglomerates which in one degree or another report on a divisional basis. Among these are Martin Marietta Corporation and The Glidden Company mentioned above. Examination of these reports indicates broad-brush resolution of these problems. Martin Marietta's report contains no information about its method for allocating extra-divisional expenses. Glidden, in computing the profits of its divisions in 1966, divides "corporate items" on the basis of "assets employed" in the division. Is this a sufficient basis? Does it ignore too readily the problems mentioned above —where costly capital is used, how research and development costs relate to the various divisions? Such allocation may mask many important characteristics necessary to sound investment analysis. In some measure all the fearsome complexities of establishing a cost justification defense in a Robinson-Patman case are transported into the disclosure arena.

One of the concerns of those pondering the problems of conglomerate reporting is litigation. In view of the rising tide of suits under Rule 10b-5 and other security enactments it is little wonder that this aspect looms large. The concern is that the additional information may be misleading or deceptive unless it is so heavily enshrouded in qualifications, definitions and caveats that it becomes meaningless and detracts from the comprehensibility of the conventional portions of the report. Whether this is a real concern will depend largely on the methods of disclosure sought to be applied and the extent to which they are qualified.[31]

There is an obverse side to this concern. Is not the *absence* of divisional reporting likely in some circumstances to give rise to litigation? Take a hypothetical case like this. A corporation has two divisions approximately equal in sales and employment of assets. One is very profitable, the other a loser. It sells the winner and continues to operate the loser. While the sale is pending or after it is consummated but before the corporation makes a disclosure of corporate—now single division—results, an investor unaware of the sharply differing profitability purchases securities from an insider or simply in the market from anyone. Is there liability on the part of the corporation or the insider for failure to disclose the very material fact that the remaining enterprise is and has been a loser?

The problem of conglomerate reporting arises at a time when under the prods of litigation, the Commission, and professional awareness, the accounting profession is making significant strides in achieving uniformity of reporting practices, thereby assisting in comparisons of competing enterprises and facilitating judgment of management. Divergences from pronouncements of the Accounting Principles Board must be disclosed and there has been considerable achievement in enunciating standards. The profession is legitimately concerned with whether while progress is being made in this sector the proposal for divisional or product-line reporting, by introducing new elements of uncertainty and opportunities for varied reporting practices, may not be a step in the opposite direction.

Any method of segmented reporting will require extensive disclosure of the methods used in allocating corporate costs and certain other items and fulsome disclaimers with respect to the conformity of the reporting

[31] A thorough and incisive analysis of the liability aspects of conglomerate disclosure by Prof. Donald E. Schwartz of Georgetown University will appear shortly in *The Business Lawyer*.

to auditing standards. A committee of the American Institute of Certified Public Accountants has strongly urged that because of the problems discussed here and others such divisional or product-line reports not be included among those to which the auditors' opinion relates. It would appear likely that this suggestion would find final acceptance since the effort to conform segmental reporting requirements to auditing practices without altering grievously the latter would be most difficult.

This discussion is not intended to express on this problem any opinion of the Subcommittee on General Accounting Problems of the American Bar Association's Committee on Federal Regulation of Securities or the author. Rather it is an attempt to spotlight the problems, summarize the multi-party dialogue to date, and suggest a need for caution and care.

Perhaps the final words for the moment should be those of Chairman Cohen before Senator Hart's Subcommittee:

> While the problems facing us are not insurmountable, they are difficult problems, and I do not believe we will find simple answers to them. Their difficulty suggests that we must proceed with deliberation and with a recognition that experience may prove to be our best guide in reaching the most appropriate solution.[32]

[32] Statement of Manuel F. Cohen to the Subcommittee on Anti-Trust and Monopoly, Committee on the Judiciary, United States Senate, September 20, 1966, pp. 1987–8.

ANDREW BARR

Conglomerate Reporting–
A View from the Securities
and Exchange Commission

The invitation to participate in this symposium on financial reporting by "conglomerate" corporations was addressed to Chairman Cohen with an impressive prospectus, including a quotation from his address before the American Institute of Certified Public Accountants in Boston over a year ago.[1] In the quoted passage a reference to a *sense of urgency* in dealing with this subject was underscored. Since that time, and for some months before, the subject has been on the agenda for consideration by trade associations and professional organizations and has been a popular topic for financial writers. And now, at this meeting, the sponsors are confident that our discussions will serve as an effective complement to the major study of the entire issue of financial reporting by "conglomerates" launched by the Financial Executives Institute.

The FEI study, which Dr. Robert Mautz of the University of Illinois is making, will meet a commitment to the SEC made by the FEI before Chairman Cohen spoke in Boston. The study is directed by an administrative comittee of the FEI, and progress is reported periodically to an advisory board composed of representatives of organizations which are interested in the success of the project. Interim reports by Dr. Mautz have appeared in the July and September 1967 issues of the *Financial Executive,* and a third appears in the current November issue. These reports deal with the subjects of "Identification of the Conglomerate Company," "Conglomerate Reporting and Data Reliability," and "Bases for More Detailed Reporting by Diversified Companies."

The diversity of interests represented by the participants in the program for today and tomorrow should serve to encourage Dr. Mautz in his

---

[1] The Securities and Exchange Commission, as a matter of policy, disclaims responsibility for any private publication by any of its employees. The views expressed herein are those of the author and do not necessarily reflect the views of the Commission or of the author's colleagues on the staff of the Commission.

work and conceivably could raise questions requiring answers before he summarizes his results. For myself, I find I am among friends of long standing even though we may not agree at all times on all accounting matters.

As background for our discussion today, a glimpse into the past may be in order. At the beginning of this century, corporate managements and independent accountants were faced with the problem of reporting on the expansion of industrial empires through vertical as well as horizontal integration. And the literature of those days seems to indicate that different kinds of enterprises were brought together under holding companies.

Montgomery dealt with the subject in the first edition of "Auditing Theory and Practice" in a chapter of ten pages on holding companies.[2] The chapter opens with the sentence, "In the face of the Sherman Act, business combinations are being formed daily." Montgomery said that the balance sheet published by a holding company of that day was "wholly devoid of the information an investor or stockholder seeks" and frequently was prepared in a misleading manner. He used even stronger language in denouncing the legal argument that the holding company should report in its profit and loss account only the dividends received from subsidiaries during the period. "This sounds well in theory," he said, "but in practice it is the argument of dishonest men." He points out that this theory of reporting permitted management to conceal losses of some subsidiaries while reporting dividends from others, thus condoning various possibilities for deceiving stockholders. Examples are cited. Montgomery concluded that "Wherever a holding company owns and controls one or more subsidiaries, the profits or losses of the subsidiaries must be stated for the same period as that of the holding company and consolidated. Any other method may lead to gross abuse."

This early and very brief discussion carries within it an endorsement of the equity method of accounting for investments in subsidiaries only recently fully supported by the Accounting Principles Board in its Opinion No. 10 through an amendment of Accounting Research Bulletin No. 51 on "Consolidated Financial Statements." Montgomery also laid down in no uncertain terms a rule of practice which the SEC found it necessary to reiterate in an amendment to the proxy rules three and one-half years ago. The amended rule in effect warns managements that too much flexibility in principles of consolidation could not be tolerated. It requires that "consolidated financial statements of the issuer and its subsidiaries shall be included in the report [to stockholders] if they are necessary to reflect adequately the financial position and results of operations of the issuer and its subsidiaries. . . ."[3]

[2] Montgomery, Robert H., "Auditing Theory and Practice," Chapter XXX, New York: The Ronald Press Company, 1913.

[3] Rule 14a-3, Securities Exchange Act of 1934.

I have started with this brief comment on consolidated statements to emphasize at the outset that despite our recognition of the growing need for information about the segments of a conglomerate enterprise, we do not underrate the continuing need for properly prepared consolidated financial statements to report the overall financial condition and results of operations of the enterprise in which the investor has an interest.

An examination of current guidelines, including Article 4 of the SEC's Regulation S-X, for the preparation of a consolidated financial statement discloses, I think, that the current consideration of reporting on the various segments of an affiliated group of companies involves an extension of a long-standing practice rather than a completely new idea. Our regulations are stated in broad terms similar to the passage I have quoted from the proxy rules. These include a warning to consider carefully the propriety of consolidating foreign operations affected by adverse conditions and a requirement that, if majority-owned subsidiaries are omitted from consolidation for valid reasons, financial statements of these omitted subsidiaries, consolidated or combined in an appropriate manner, shall be filed if essential to a properly summarized presentation of the facts. We endorse the equity method of accounting in the parent and consolidated statements for such omitted subsidiaries. With certain exceptions, the rules prohibit inclusion of insurance companies and banks in consolidation with industrial and commercial companies. If material, separate or combined statements, as appropriate, of such companies are required. There are differences of opinion in accounting circles as to when captive finance companies should be included. Current AICPA bulletins support our view that real estate companies which own property used by the parent should be included in consolidation. Many of the large finance companies have diversified their operations by acquiring manufacturing and merchandising companies. The separate character of these companies has been disclosed for many years—long before the present active discussion of the "conglomerate" company problem.

Experience in requiring compliance with the Commission's existing reporting requirements indicates the need for our present study. A report on Form 8-K under the Securities Exchange Act of 1934 is required to be filed upon the occurrence of certain events. One of these events is the acquisition of a business. If material with respect to the registrant, financial statements for the acquired business must be furnished. Considerable resistance to furnishing such financials is expressed when the acquisition is of a closely held single-product company, often quite different from the acquiring company's business. It is argued that only at this one time will details of the operations of the single-product business ever be disclosed, because after acquisition its operations will be included in the consolidated financial statements. The purpose of the disclosure requirement, of course, is to provide information for the stockholders of the acquiring company by which they may judge the actions of their management. The present materiality test here is 15 percent of assets or revenues of the registrant. A current proposal would reduce this to 10 percent. Should continued disclosure of the operations of the acquired company be required under some similar tests?

Rules under the Securities Exchange Act also require the filing of semiannual reports of profit and loss and earned surplus information. The rules are pursuant to a provision of the act which was first implemented at the close of World War II to require at that time the reporting only of gross revenues as an indication of the effect on the company of the end of the war. Later, financial analysts sought interim net income as well as revenues. Noting that in many cases as volume of business went up net income went down, the Commission rescinded as inadequate the requirement for volume-only reports and adopted requirements for the present form of a simple midyear income statement. This experience is pertinent to our present inquiry, as I will show in a few moments.

Registration Forms 10 and S-1 require the registrants to give a description of the business. Similar instructions under both forms specify that "If the business consists of the production or distribution of different kinds of products or the rendering of different kinds of services, indicate, insofar as practicable, the relative importance of each product or service or class of similar products or services which contributed 15 percent or more to the gross volume of business done during the last fiscal year." It should be noted here that at the end of 1966 the Financial Executives Institute urged its members to give a breakdown of sales in their reports to stockholders. Our review of the 1966 reports showed a substantial improvement in the disclosure of such data over the prior year. It should also be noted that, whereas our instruction in these forms refers to the last fiscal year, prospectuses (and reports to stockholders as well) often include tables showing the composition of sales by major product lines for a period of years.

If you will recall my reference to the inadequacy of reporting sales alone, certain words in the Form 10 and Form S-1 instructions become significant. The instruction calls for an indication, "insofar as practicable," of "the relative importance of each product or service or class of similar products or services. . . ." Except by a fortunate coincidence sales alone will not answer this question of relative importance. Hence the staff and, as I have observed, enlightened managements in their reports to stockholders have sought to answer this question in some manner. Some examples may demonstrate the point, although it hardly needs elaborate discussion.

The January 3, 1967, edition of the *Wall Street Journal* carried a "Letter to Stockholders" from Wilson & Co., Inc. which included a table identical to the one in the report to stockholders issued a week later. This table, as given below, was in each case introduced by a statement that each of the three divisions of the company had higher sales and earnings than the year before:

| | MILLIONS | | | |
| | 1966 | | 1965 | |
	Sales	Net Earnings	Sales	Net Earnings
Meat and Food Products	$875	$ 7.7	$731	$4.9
Athletic Goods	80	3.7	73	3.1
Chemical Industries	36	1.5	29	1.3
	$991	$12.9	$833	$9.3

A recent prospectus includes information in table and text which can be reported in a single table for quicker comprehension:

Percentages of total dollar sales of principal product groupings and contributions of such product groupings to consolidated net income were:

Product Group (Described in text)	1964		1965		1966	
	Sales	Income	Sales	Income	Sales	Income
A	56%	80%	56%	83%	48%	70%
B	26%	20%	24%	10%	22%	18%
C	18%	0%	20%	7%	30%	12%

This example warrants further comment. The question of consistency and comparability of financial statements from year to year for each company and for companies in the same industry is a popular subject for discussion today—as it has been for about as long as I can remember. This example is taken from one company in over sixty in its very important industry which file financial statements with the Commission. I doubt very much if any two of these companies are enough alike to say that the same breakdown would be pertinent to each. Individual characteristics of each should be brought out for the financial analyst and investor to consider. Tables of figures without the basis for informed judgment are not likely to be useful.

Just in case it has not come to your attention, in England the Companies Act of 1967 amends prior acts to require that directors' reports in respect of financial years ending on or after the 27th of July, 1968, include:

"*Analysis of turnover and profit or loss before taxation* of the company, or in the case of a holding company submitting consolidated accounts, of the group, between substantially different classes of business, stating, unless turnover is not required to be disclosed in the accounts [instructions omitted]:

   a. the proportions in which the turnover is divided amongst those classes (describing them)

   b. the extent or approximate extent (expressed in monetary terms) to which, in the opinion of the directors, each class of business has contributed to, or restricted, the profit or loss of the company for the year before taxation." [4]

The topic before us has attracted a great deal of attention and vigorous favorable as well as adverse comment. Since my role here today is to support a reasonable interpretation of our disclosure requirements, which we deem to require some clarification as to conglomerate companies, some supporting comment may be appropriate here.

We have noted many comments citing the benefits of and the need for additional disclosures by diversified companies, which were made by a rather wide range of writers. These include corporation executives, financial analysts, professors, public accountants, and individual investors, as well as many general financial writers.

For the most part, as might be expected, the comments have stressed the needs of investors for the additional information. The following, by an investment analyst, is illustrative:

"... the conventional tools of investment analysis fail to provide adequate answers to an investor or stockholder when dealing with a conglomerate company which does not disclose major divisional operations. To assess the individual importance of a hodgepodge of products and their impact on sales and earnings of a company is often impossible without proper published information." [5]

On the other hand some corporate executives have indicated that they believe their corporations also benefit by such disclosure. A financial vice president of a company that provides an informative breakdown of net income stated that this allocation "has been extremely helpful to me in building relationships with security analysts." He indicated that he was convinced that the breakdown is of value to the individual investor as well as to the professional analyst, and said: "We would rather provide a fair presentation of the data than have him guess. We have found that it builds a certain amount of confidence."

The Commission's record in this matter has been stated repeatedly

[4] See "Guide to the Accounting Requirements of The Companies Acts 1948–1967," page 25, Published for the General Educational Trust of the Institute of Chartered Accountants in England and Wales by Gee & Co. (Publishers) Limited, London, England.

[5] "Economic Concentration," Hearings before the Subcommittee on Anti-Trust and Monopoly, Committee on the Judiciary, United States Senate, Part 4, p. 1706.

at various professional meetings—most recently at the annual meeting of the Financial Executives Institute in Montreal. On that occasion I dealt with a few misconceptions of our views which have come to our attention. Since those remarks appear in the November issue of the *Financial Executive* they need not be repeated here.

In 1965 the Commission responded to an inquiry from Senator Philip A. Hart, Chairman, Subcommittee on Anti-Trust and Monopoly of the Committee on the Judiciary. This response, which covers some of the matters I have mentioned this morning as well as a brief recital of some of the accounting problems involved in product-line reporting, may be found at page 1069 of Part 2 of the record of hearings of this subcommittee published under the title of "Economic Concentration." Chairman Cohen, when called to testify before Senator Hart's subcommittee on September 20, 1966, referred to this memorandum and then said:

> "Up to now, however, except in the case of companies selling both goods and services, we have had no general requirement that conglomerate companies break down their financial statements to show results of operations for their different divisions. As our 1965 memorandum set forth, there are a number of reasons why we did not do so. But changes have been occurring recently which have made it necessary for us to reconsider our requirements in this area despite the difficulties we will have to face.
>
> "The most important change, as you are of course well aware, is the growing tendency toward absorption of separate industrial enterprises into large conglomerate companies. Each time one of these enterprises is absorbed, and ceases to publish separate financial statements, the available information about the industry in which that enterprise is engaged is correspondingly reduced. Acceleration of the trend toward absorption of these independent enterprises makes it increasingly difficult for investors and others to draw intelligent conclusions about the affairs and prospects of companies in the particular industries and this, of course, applies even to the conglomerate companies or to independent companies. Now, this creates a very real threat to the ability of independent investors to reach informed investment decisions, which Congress has recognized as a basic prerequisite to a healthy securities market and which philosophy underlies all of the securities statutes administered by the Commission." [6]

This states the SEC's view.

[6] "Economic Concentration," *op. cit.*, Part 5, p. 1983.

JOHN M. BLAIR

Antitrust Implications

of

Conglomerate Reporting

INTRODUCTION I have been asked to address myself to the question of the need for divisional reporting from the antitrust point of view. That need stems from the existence and, in recent years, the rapid growth of the conglomerate corporation.

In the context of industry structure the term "conglomerate" was first used to designate a particular type of merger. It was used to refer to the "all other" category of acquisitions, i.e., those which are neither horizontal (where the acquiring and the acquired firms produce the same product) nor vertical (those where the products involved are in the same stream of production and distribution). Gradually the term has also come to be used as descriptive of the multi-industry firm itself—typically a very large enterprise engaged in a variety of different industries which have little, if any, relationship to each other.

If a conglomerate possesses substantial monopoly power in one or more of the industries in which it operates, it is in a position to engage in a practice which can probably best be referred to as "cross-subsidization."[1] This is the use of profits obtained in industries in which it possesses substantial monopoly power to subsidize sales in competitive industries made at a loss or at an abnormally low profit.[2]

Such a practice is destructive to competition since it makes the plight of the single-line producer all but impossible. Even though in his own industry he were more efficient than the conglomerate, there is little point in pursuing the course of action held out by classical theory, i.e., reducing his

[1] The same practice has been referred to as "product discrimination" (John M. Blair, "The Conglomerate Merger in Economics and Law," *Georgetown Law Review*, Summer 1958); and as a form of "price discrimination" (Carl Kaysen, *United States v. United Shoe Machinery Corp.*, 1956, p. 127). The use of the latter term, "price discrimination," may be confusing since in its usual sense it refers to sales of a given product to different purchasers at different prices.
[2] Profits could be considered to be abnormally low if they were substantially below what would have been yielded if the firm had behaved as a competitive supplier in view of the market's prevailing cost and demand factors.

price to reflect his greater efficiency, since his price reduction would only be matched or exceeded by a firm which has already manifested a willingness to accept losses. Moreover, any attempt by the single-line producer to diversify into some other field would be hindered by a price level in his own industry which prevents both the retention of earnings and the attraction of capital from the outside.

ANTITRUST INTEREST IN DIVISIONAL REPORTING

The interest in divisional reporting of those concerned with antitrust (at least of those concerned with antitrust who are also concerned with the conglomerate problem) stems from the need to know whether, where and the extent to which conglomerate firms are engaging in cross-subsidization. At this point it should be emphasized that this practice does not constitute the whole of the concern over conglomerate expansion from an antitrust standpoint. Even if cross-subsidization were nonexistent or of minimal proportions, competition could still be lessened by virtue of the awareness on the part of the single-line producers that if they behaved in a more competitive fashion they could be subject to retaliation by a firm which in their industry could operate at a loss without materially affecting its overall profit showings. Competition could also be lessened by reciprocal arrangements among conglomerates which have the effect of denying other firms access to important markets. And it could be lessened by the unwillingness of two (or more) conglomerates who confront each other in a number of separate industries to initiate a competitive move in any one of those industries since to do so would invite retaliation from the other conglomerate in different industries in which they were both engaged.

But at least one of the ways by which competition can be lessened through conglomerate expansion will remain largely out of sight (though hopefully not out of mind) unless and until a meaningful program of divisional reporting for large conglomerate firms is put into effect.

Without divisional reporting, our knowledge of cross-subsidization is, to put it mildly, fragmentary. To some observers, this has meant that the practice is nonexistent—a figment of the imagination of those who seek to besmirch the escutcheon of corporate management.[3] To others it merely signifies the understandable reluctance of corporate officials to provide the antitrust agencies with proof of a possibly unlawful practice,[4] or dissident stockholders with evidence of high-level mismanagement. Nonetheless, despite these understandable reasons for non-disclosure, indications of cross-subsidization do on occasion come to the surface. To give some concreteness to this analysis, the practice can be illustrated by the postwar expansion of the nation's largest firm into a number of industries which are at best only distantly related and by the marked change which has taken place in the structure of the electric appliance industry.

[3] Cf., e.g., Donald F. Turner, "Conglomerate Mergers and Section 7 of the Clayton Act," *Harvard Law Review*, May 1965.

[4] Cf. *U.S. v. Griffith*, 334 U.S. 100 (1948); *U.S. v. United Shoe Machinery Corp.*, 110 F. Supp., 295 (D. Mass. 1953).

**GENERAL MOTORS'
CONGLOMERATE
EXPANSION**

Much of the Senate Anti-Trust Subcommittee's first report on automobiles (the 1956 report) was concerned with the conglomerate nature of General Motors' expansion into the diesel locomotive, bus, and earth-moving machinery industries. The success of G.M.'s expansion into these industries was attributed in no small part to the company's monopolistic power and profits flowing from its controlling position in the manufacture and financing of automobiles. The report stated:

> In both buses and diesel locomotives it was shown that General Motors was able to give liberal financing terms through its financial affiliates, General Motors Acceptance Corp. (GMAC) and Yellow Manufacturing Acceptance Corp. (YMAC), which was of inestimable advantage in securing a favored market position.
>
> *　*　*
>
> Competition was seriously disadvantaged by the ability of General Motors to make capital investments in bus purchasers—both transit and intercity—and thus secure certain preferences. Various types of exclusive contracts have apparently been utilized by the corporation in its climb to power. Some of these, which gave it advantages over its competitors were held by a court to be part of a plan in violation of the antitrust laws.
>
> *　*　*
>
> Railroads which were purchasers of buses and locomotives were also beneficiaries of General Motors' freight shipments. It was claimed that railroads "naturally" favored such a good freight customer in making their own purchases. The tremendous financial resources of both General Motors and GMAC, which were deposited in banks in 157 cities throughout the United States, gave it great influence.
>
> *　*　*
>
> GMAC is also a good customer of banks, having borrowed up to the legal limit from almost every major bank in the country. It was claimed that directors of banks who also served on the boards of bus purchasers were inclined to favor General Motors over its competitors. Both in buses and diesel locomotives, there was evidence that reciprocity gave General Motors advantages.
>
> *　*　*
>
> In the acquisition of the Euclid Road Machinery Co., General Motors most recently utilized its financial ability to enter an industry by purchase, even though it was capable of doing so by internal expansion. . . . Although competition was affected by the vertical acquisition of a market for G.M. diesel engines, the conglomerate aspect of the merger raised the more serious questions.[5]

On the basis of information supplied by General Motors, it was estimated in the subcommittee's 1958 report that 35 percent of the company's total sales and costs related at that time to activities other than the production and sale of automobiles and trucks.[6] The report also revealed that over

[5] *A Study of the Antitrust Laws*—"Bigness and Concentration of Economic Power—A Case Study of General Motors Corporation" (S. Report 1879, 84th Cong., 2d. Sess.) pp. 10–11.
[6] U.S. Senate Subcommittee on Anti-Trust and Monopoly, "Administered Prices, Automobiles" (85th Cong., 2d. Sess.) pp. 25–26.

the period of 1946–1957 G.M. incurred sporadic losses in certain operating divisions. In one year, for example, its truck division suffered losses amounting to 1.8 percent of sales.[7] G.M.'s president suffered a lapse of memory when confronted with Senator Kefauver's question: "Just as an example, years ago didn't you get into a fight in the truck industry with other competitors, and for a while you operated your truck industry at a loss? You made that up by the very substantial amounts you earned in your other operations." [8] A subsequent letter from the company confirmed this loss, which is attributed to an "accounting writeoff." [9] Referring to the period 1946–1957, the company stated that "for the aggregate period of 12 years . . . every General Motors division operated at a profit." [10] Noting that 12 years is not a customary accounting period, the report observed: "The smaller single-line company competing with General Motors in any one of its industries must be concerned with what has happened to its profits in the last quarter, the last 6 months, the last year. It is the exceptional small entrepreneur who need concern himself only with his return in terms of an aggregate for a 12-year period." [11]

The report then went on to note the rapidity with which concentration tended to rise following the entrance of G.M. into an industry:

> An examination of this subcommittee's hearings in 1955 show, however, that by 1954, General Motors shipped 100% of all road freight and road passenger diesel locomotives sold in the United States. The physical volume, of course, had greatly lessened by 1954 since almost complete dieselization of the railroad industry had been accomplished by 1952. The same situation occurred in connection with diesel switchers. In 1950—the peak year in its history—there were 4,174 switchers ordered in this country, and General Motors' share was 48% of switchers and 57% of road switchers. By 1954, total orders had been reduced to 983, but General Motors' portion of the business had risen to 60% and 74%, respectively.

> ❋   ❋   ❋

> An increase likewise occurred in the company's share of the motorbus market. In 1950 its sales amounted to 46% of the total market; a steady climb resulted in a 78% share by 1954, and by 1955 the company manufactured approximately 85% of the new buses delivered in the United States.[12]

ELECTRICAL APPLIANCES   Among the 400-odd manufacturing industries, few have experienced a more rapid increase in concentration since World War II than electrical appliances. A widely-defined area, it embraces numerous different products with different uses which are in no way substitutable for each other. Ranging from $2 fans to $500 freezers, its products have in common only the

---

[7] *Ibid.*, p. 30.
[8] *Idem.*
[9] *Idem.*
[10] *Ibid.*, p. 30.
[11] *Idem.*
[12] *Ibid.*, p. 33.

characteristics of being durable goods, powered by electricity, and customarily used in the home. Although the industry is defined so broadly as to have little meaning, concentration ratios fortunately are available for most of its individual product classes. Shown below are the shares of the four leading producers for seven different types of electric appliances, which account for more than three-fifths of the total shipments of all electric appliances:

CONCENTRATION IN SELECTED ELECTRIC APPLIANCES, 1954, 1958 AND 1963

SIC Class	Product	Concentration Ratios 4 Largest Companies			Change: % Points	
		1954	1958	1963	1954–58	1954–63
36322	Home and farm freezers	44%	58%	63%	14	19
36321	Household refrigerators	62	73	76	11	14
3633	Household laundry equipment	58	67	71	9	13
36341	Electric fans, ex. industrial	46	54	46	8	0
	Vacuum cleaners 1	55	59	n.a.	4	—
36360	Sewing machines	76	D	82	—	6
36391	Household water heaters, elec.	39	37	40	–2	1

D Withheld to avoid disclosure of individual company figures; concentration ratios for 8 largest companies: 89 in 1954; 92 in 1958.

1 Household vacuum cleaners (36350) and commercial and industrial vacuum cleaners (35840) combined for 1958 to provide a comparable figure with the 1954 product class 3584.

Source: Concentration in Manufacturing Industry, 1958, Part 1, Table 4; Concentration in Manufacturing Industry, 1963, Part 1, Table 4.

Most of the increases, as can be seen, took place during the mid-fifties. The share held by the four largest producers of home and farm freezers registered a precipitous advance—from 44 percent in 1954 to 58 percent in 1958. Almost as large was the increase in household refrigerators—from 62 percent to 73 percent. During these four years the concentration ratio rose by 9 percentage points in household laundry equipment, while an increase of 8 percentage points was registered by electric fans. In sewing machines, the four largest companies in 1954 held 76 percent, while their share could not be revealed in 1958 because of the disclosure rule; during the same period the share held by the eight largest companies rose from 89 to 92 percent.

According to the trade press, the mid-fifties was a period of recurring weaknesses in the market. The major producers apparently did not limit supplies, as a result of which inventories accumulated and prices weakened. Paradoxically, at the same time that the market was reported to be glutted by "overcapacity," the largest and most diversified producers were making substantial expansions in their capacity. In January, 1956, General Electric, the industry's largest producer, was reported to be lowering the prices of its small appliances "up to 30 percent," featuring a reduction in the price of vacuum cleaners from $69.95 to $49.95. The purpose of the price change, it was stated, was to allow G.E. to promote new products "at more realistic prices." [13] A month later it was reported that four firms, including Westinghouse, would reduce their prices of these appliances "to stabilize the appliance industry." [14] Several months later an official of a substantial but smaller company, Borg-Warner, reacted critically to these price reductions, stating:

> In an effort to buy an out-of-proportionate share of the market, a few selfish manufacturers have set off a whole chain of wheeling and dealing price merchandising tactics. A price—any price—below price of competition is their price to dealers.[15]

Between the fourth quarter of 1954 and the fourth quarter of 1960 the Wholesale Price Index rose 9.1 percent, the price index for consumer durable goods increased 8.7 percent, and the index for metals and metal products advanced 17.3 percent. In contrast, the prices of G.E. major appliances registered pronounced decreases, ranging from 9 percent for free-standing ranges to 27 percent for standard 10-cubic-foot freezers. Built-in ranges, DeLuxe refrigerators and 13-foot freezers were reduced by 19 percent. Prices of its refrigerators, freezers and washers were reduced between 1954–57 and again between 1957–60. Substantial reductions were made in the price of G.E. ranges between 1954 and 1957.

This was also a period of a wholesale exodus of single-line manufacturers—large and small—from the industry. Articles in the trade press reflected a premonition that the future of the industry lay only with the large conglomerate firms, for whom appliance manufacturing constitutes only a small part of their business. Thus, in late 1956, *Retailing Daily* featured a front-page article which proclaimed, "The ever-changing profile of the major appliance industry suffered the most radical alteration in many a day" with the shutdown of one firm and the sale of another, which climaxed "24 months of shuffling, shifting, buying and selling. . . ." [16] The article continued, ". . . the result of all the shifting within the industry is one of reducing the number of competitive brands on the market. Like a poker game, apparently, the more players that can be knocked out of a hand, the greater is the possibility of winning." [17]

Whirlpool-Seeger's president was quoted as saying that of the twenty-six independent laundry manufacturers in 1940, ten had merged into full-line companies, eight had been liquidated or gone into bankruptcy, leaving

---

13 *Appliance Manufacturer*, January 1956.

14 *Ibid.*, February 1956.

15 *Appliance Manufacturer*, July 1956.

16 Jerry Lansky, "C-B Moves Climax Appliance Shuffle," *Retailing Daily* (now *Home Furnishing Daily*), Nov. 15, 1956, p. 1.

17 *Idem.*

only eight still in business. He was also quoted to the effect that among the advantages of the "full-line company" is its ability *to subsidize a line of appliances* in a given market or at a given season." [18]

Between 1954 and 1961, sixty formerly independent appliance manufacturers disappeared through mergers and acquisitions. More than half the casualties occurred in 1955 and 1956, during which period seven home laundry manufacturers and seven refrigerator or freezer manufacturers, as well as three electric range manufacturers, were eliminated through merger. A good number of these firms were sizable enterprises which could reasonably be expected to have attained the available economies of scale and had long-established and well-known trade names. Among the disappearances were firms with such well-known names—which either vanished entirely or have been used for prestige purposes by an acquiring company—as "Deepfreeze," "York," "Welbilt," "Bendix," "Speed Queen," "Easy," "Eureka," "Jordan," "Dormeyer," "Servel," "Universal," "Ever Bright," and "Philco."

The result of this period of turmoil was that a few large conglomerate corporations, notably General Electric, and to a lesser extent General Motors and Westinghouse, ended up with substantial control over most of the industry's product lines. This can be seen from the attached table, which is based upon a market survey conducted by *Look* magazine in 1961; as a service to advertisers, this survey showed market shares by individual companies.[19]

Of the eight major appliances surveyed by *Look*, General Electric had the largest market share in no less than five—ranges, refrigerators, clothes dryers, water heaters, and dishwashers. In two of the remaining products it had the second largest share—freezers and automatic clothes washers—while in the remaining product it was the third leading producer. In the five products in which it was the leading producer, G.E.'s share ranged from

[18] *Retailing Daily*, Nov. 15, 1956, p. 34 (emphasis added).

[19] For the *Look National Survey*, Audits & Surveys Co. used a multi-stage area probability sampling technique, with interviews conducted in 4,808 households for the 1959 survey and 5,292 households for the 1961 survey. The results are subject to the qualifications that attach to any sample survey; however, the results, which are in terms of "acquired new," compare closely with the Census data, as can be seen below:

Product	4 Largest Companies	
	Census 1958	Look Survey 1959–60
Household ranges, electric	67	74
Household mechanical washing machines, dryers and washer-dryer combinations	68	73 [a] 71 [b]
Vacuum cleaners	64	60
Water heaters	37	42
Household refrigerators, electric	73	64

[a] Automatic clothes washers.
[b] Electric clothes dryers.

FOUR LEADING COMPANIES IN APPLIANCE MANUFACTURING, 1959–60

Appliance	Manufacturer	Households Acquiring New in 1959–60	
Vacuum cleaners	Hoover Co.	21%	
	Electrolux Corp.	16	
	General Electric Co.	13	
	Kirby	10	60
Electric refrig. household mech.	General Electric Co.	24	
	General Motors Corp.	17	
	Whirlpool	14	
	Borg-Warner	9	64
Home and farm freezers	Whirlpool	19	
	General Electric Co.	9	
	General Motors Corp.	9	
	Westinghouse Electric Corp.	6	44
Dishwashing . . . and other service machinery n.e.c.	General Electric Co.	36	
	Hobart Mfg. Co.	18	
	Whirlpool	13	
	General Motors Corp.	11	79
Household mechanical washing machines	Whirlpool	32	
	General Electric Co.	21	
	General Motors Corp.	11	
	Maytag Co.	8	73
Household ranges, electric	General Electric Co.	40	
	General Motors Corp.	15	
	Westinghouse Electric Corp.	10	
	Whirlpool	9	74
Household water heaters, electric	General Electric Co.	32	
	Rheem Mfg. Co.	6	
	Westinghouse Electric Corp.	2	
	General Motors Corp.	2	
	A. O. Smith Corp.	2	42
Electric clothes dryers	General Electric Co.	27	
	Whirlpool	19	
	Westinghouse Electric Corp.	13	
	General Motors Corp.	13	71

Source: Look National Survey, 1961.

24 percent (refrigerators) to 40 percent (electric ranges), while in the three remaining products it held from 9 to 21 percent. General Motors was the second largest producer of refrigerators (17 percent and of ranges (15 percent), the third largest producer of washing machines (11 percent) and of freezers (9 percent), and in addition was the fourth largest in dryers (13 percent), dishwashers (11 percent), and electric water heaters (2 percent). Westinghouse appears as the third largest producer of ranges (10 percent), clothes dryers (13 percent), and electric water heaters (2 percent), and the fourth largest in freezers (6 percent).

To what extent, if at all, were the increases in concentration the result of cross-subsidization by the largest producers? Without divisional reporting we, of course, do not know. But the possibility that such was the case is suggested by the writings of T. K. Quinn, former chairman of G.E.'s sales committee, the G.E. Contracts Corp., vice-chairman of the General Electric Supply Corp., and operating head of its appliance business. Holding that the company had long followed a policy of using profits from its "monopoly lines" to drive out competition in other lines, Mr. Quinn wrote that the "secret" of G.E.'s predominance and growth rested upon two foundations:

1. As a J. P. Morgan combine originally (like General Motors and U.S. Steel) it had abundant capital, including access, through Morgan, to life insurance funds.
2. It had high-profit, monopoly lines which enabled it to finance other lines until they, too, could reach volumes that would assure their continuance on a self-supporting and profitable basis.

Referring to the latter he went on to state:

Notable among these lines was the incandescent electric lamp bulb monopoly. G.E.'s net profit in its lamp department at times approximated 50% of investment. . . .
It was from its lamp profits that General Electric financed its entry into the home appliance field. . . . There was no purpose or advantage of efficiency involved.[20]

In this connection it should be observed that the manufacture of electric lamps is one of the most highly-concentrated industries in the country, with the four largest producers regularly accounting for more than 90 percent of the output. According to data put into the Court record in the 1953 case, General Electric, alone, accounted for approximately 55 percent and Westinghouse for 25 percent of lamp sales.[21] Another probable source of monopoly profits was heavy electrical machinery; it was during this same period that General Electric, Westinghouse, and most of the other pro-

[20] T. K. Quinn, *Unconscious Public Enemies*, Citadel Press, 1962, pp. 112–114.
[21] *U.S. v. General Electric Co. et al.*, 115 F. Supp. 835, 882–883, Appendix Tables 1 & 2.

ducers were engaged in a far-reaching—and shockingly illegal—conspiracy, the purpose of which was, of course, to enhance prices.[22]

Another possible indication lies in the vigor with which G.E., following its conviction in the 1960 "Philadelphia" conspiracy case, opposed an attempt by the Department of Justice to enjoin the use of what has been described here as "cross-subsidization." The Department was apprehensive that G.E. and the other large companies would use their conviction for failing to compete as a pretext for competing by sales-below-costs against smaller rivals. To prevent such an eventuality, the Department attempted to write an "unreasonably low" price prohibition into the consent orders. This clause was actually signed by one defendant company [23] while four others, including Westinghouse, initially gave assurances of their acceptance.

But, preferring the possibility of a court battle, General Electric refused to sign, contending that the language was vague and would tend to stifle rather than encourage competition. For a company which during its lifetime had run afoul of the antitrust laws on so many occasions, this concern with the cause of competition was rather unexpected. Moreover, having just been convicted for engaging in the most egregious price-fixing conspiracy of modern times, resulting in the imprisonment of several of its top officials, one would not have thought that G.E. would have been eager to precipitate in still another court battle—unless the practice involved was of key importance to its corporate strategy. For reasons that have never been too clear the Justice Department quietly dropped the provision from the final decree.

LIMITATIONS AND USES OF DIVISIONAL REPORTING

That a multi-product firm will have differing profit rates in the different industries in which it is engaged is almost inevitable and, in itself, constitutes no particular cause for concern. As Kaysen has observed, "In general, it can be said that discrimination of the kind discussed here is never entirely absent in any actual market, especially one in which the typical seller produces many products under conditions of common overhead costs of various

[22] For an illustration of their success in terms of both listed and realized prices, see John M. Blair, "Administered Prices & Oligopolistic Inflation—A Reply", *Journal of Business*, January 1964, p. 75.

[23] C. H. Wheeler Manufacturing Co., Civil Action #28,229, filed May 22, 1961 in the U. S. District Court for the Eastern District of Pennsylvania. The provision which was so obnoxious to G.E. appeared as follows:

Defendant . . . is enjoined and restrained from, directly or indirectly:

* * *

(F) Selling condensers at unreasonably low prices with the purpose or intent, or where the effect is, or where there is a reasonable probability that the effect will be, substantially to injure, suppress or stifle competition or tend to create a monopoly; provided, however, that in any proceeding for civil contempt based upon an alleged violation of this subsection (F) in which the plaintiff shall have sustained its burden of proving that the defendant in such proceeding has made sales which would violate this subsection (F) if such sales were at unreasonably low prices, the burden of proof shall be upon such defendent to establish that it did not sell such condensers at unreasonably low prices.

types." [24] In one or more of the industries in which it is engaged, the conglomerate firm may be sustaining actual losses under circumstances which pose no dangers to competition. Thus, when operations within a given industry which otherwise would be profitable are transformed into losses by a decline in demand, an unfavorable reaction to a new product, or any of a multitude of circumstances beyond the control of management, the effects on the industry's structure are likely to be short-lived and devoid of any serious consequences to competition.

Moreover, the losses may be due to nothing more than inefficiency. It has long been recognized that of all forms of acquisitions, the entrance into industries which are unrelated to the field of the acquiring firm offers the least potential for economies and the greatest for diseconomies. At some point the conglomerate which has entered a new field may decide to cut its losses and withdraw from the industry. Such indeed occurred in the glass fiber industry into which several of the nation's largest firms expanded, only to withdraw when it had become painfully apparent that they were unable to master the production and marketing intricacies of this new technology. If the operations of the single-line companies continue to be profitable while the conglomerate is losing money, the conglomerate's poor performance is probably due only to inefficiency. But what if the price structure is such that in an industry in which demand is not falling, the conglomerate as well as the single-line producers are losing money? Having no other sources of profits, the latter would presumably be withdrawing from the industry, either through bankruptcy or acquisition. If the conglomerate elected to "stick with it," the result would logically be an increase in concentration and specifically its share of the industry. That such a set of circumstances is not just the product of imagination but actually takes place in the real world is suggested by the experience of the electrical appliance industry.

The danger to competition thus arises when there is a *combination* of factors, which may be summarized as follows:

1. The conglomerate is in possession of substantial monopoly power in one or more of the industries in which it is engaged;
2. Any losses (or abnormally low profits) which it incurs in one or more of such industries is *not* an episodic occurrence, beyond the control of management, but continues over a period of time;
3. Such losses have only a minor effect on the corporation's overall financial showings;
4. The losses are not merely the product of inefficiency;
5. Nor can they be explained on the basis of declines in demand or costs; and

[24] Carl Kaysen, *United States v. United Shoe Machinery Corp.*, 1956, p. 127.

6. There are indications that the industry is becoming increasingly concentrated, as revealed by concentration statistics, data on disappearances and acquisitions, and general information in the trade press.

Obviously, most losses reported under a program of divisional reporting would therefore fall far short of constituting evidence of antitrust violation. Only those losses incurred in the context of the combination of the factors set forth above should properly be regarded as a cause for concern. But unless they are so regarded, there is no reason why what took place in the appliance industry should not occur in any number of other industries as well.

Already, conglomerate mergers have made a profound impression on the structure of industry. The share of total value added by manufacture accounted for by the 200 largest manufacturing companies increased from 30 percent in 1947 to 41 percent in 1963. Inasmuch as the number (and importance) of the *individual* industries in which concentration rose was about equally matched by the number in which it decreased, most of this rise in overall concentration must have been due to conglomerate expansion. From an antitrust point of view, this is perhaps the most compelling reason for the institution of divisional reporting by large, conglomerate corporations.

DUDLEY E. BROWNE

Discussion of SEC

and

Antitrust Viewpoints

In the two preceding papers, Andrew Barr explained the need for product-line reporting as a means to enhance the reliability of investment judgments in the securities market, and John Blair has established that the need for product-line reporting also exists for government investigators in the field of antitrust. A sound case for increased disclosure was made by both of these gentlemen, and, as Mr. Barr has pointed out, there seems to be substantial agreement among a variety of interested parties that such added disclosure is warranted.

As my personal contribution to the spirit of ecumenical give-and-take, which I trust will distinguish our dialogue at this symposium, I should like to open my remarks by conceding to the proponents of product-line reporting that it should be in the corporation's long-run interest to disclose information regarding sales and earnings of segments of the business.

Having made this concession, and thereby establishing my claim as a dispassionate and eminently reasonable representative from industry, I should now like to discuss certain provisos I must stipulate with respect to how industry is to furnish this information.

But before I enumerate these provisos, it might be helpful if I outlined briefly some of the work the Financial Executives Research Foundation has been doing in the area of financial reporting by conglomerate companies. I was president of the Foundation when this study was launched, and since then I have been following Professor Bob Mautz' progress with great interest. I am certain that most of you have also tried to keep current with this study. What Professor Mautz has reported to date, in my opinion, serves to identify some of the major issues that one must face in determining how to be responsible to this call for increased disclosure of segmented reporting for conglomerates.

In his July, 1967, article in *Financial Executive*, for example, he offered us a tentative definition of the conglomerate company

". . . as one which, because it is managerially decentralized, or lacks operational integration, or has diversified markets, may experience internally varying rates of profitability, degrees of risk, and opportunities for growth."

To which he adds the following constraint:

"Only those internal variations which are of sufficient magnitude to be material to investment decisions qualify a company as conglomerate."

The article, itself, was a thorough reconstruction of the painstaking and well considered analysis that led the author to these tentative conclusions.

In his September article in *Financial Executive*, Professor Mautz addressed himself to the problems of data reliability that are inherent to providing segmented reporting. Among these problems, he noted that the allocation of common costs is founded on subjective determinations. Furthermore, he stated that the allocation of costs among segments raises questions as to applicable time periods and units of product. These are internally defined components, he pointed out; and, as such, they may or may not mean to outsiders what they mean to those inside the company.

This led to the inquiry as to whether subjectivity in common cost allocations can be eliminated or at least reduced to acceptable proportions. After considering the disadvantages of establishing "required, arbitrary allocation bases" and the dilemma the independent auditors would face if they were obligated to express their opinions on cost allocations among segments of companies, in the absence of any generally accepted accounting principles at this level of accounting, Professor Mautz reached the conclusion that neither approach offered a satisfactory solution at this time.

Then he explored the possible use of the "defined profit" for reducing subjectivity. This method, he believes, warrants careful examination before any final answer can be given to its usefulness. He listed several examples that illustrate how difficult and potentially dangerous this approach might be.

The beauty of "defined profit" is that it defines profit at a higher level on the typical income statement than the last line thereof, so that the higher you move on the income statement the less problems you have with arbitrary allocations of expenses. This would include the items typically treated as period costs, such as research and development expenses, general and administrative overhead, interest costs, and so forth. However, whether such a presentation reflecting distorted profitability would answer more questions than it would create is a moot question.

Another problem area cited by Professor Mauntz in this article is that of intracompany transfers of materials and services. Here he reminded us that such transfers, taking place within a conglomerate company, lack the degree of objectivity of external transactions, and so there is no assurance that the transfer prices are realistic in the sense of having met any market test.

At the end of his September article, Professor Mautz advanced the following tentative conclusions:

1. Management must have available to it information which could be misleading if supplied to others less well acquainted with the company and the purposes for which the information was supplied.
2. Common costs and intracompany pricing pose particularly difficult problems in the preparation of operating reports for segments of companies.
3. A possible solution to common cost allocation problems is offered by the "defined profit" approach which suggests that only direct costs be matched with revenues in segment operating statements.
4. The relative importance of common costs in divisional reporting tends to decrease as the breadth of the reporting divisions is increased.
5. The influence of intracompany pricing may be of so little consequence in the reports of disparate components that such influence is no serious deterrent to the presentation of operating data for such components.

In addition to his published reports, Professor Mautz has also shared his understanding of these problems with professional groups at programs such as the one we are having here today. At the 36th Annual International Conference of the Financial Executives Institute, which recently convened in Montreal, he raised the question: Are conglomerates a peculiar sort of investment situation? His answer, he stated, insofar as the research was concerned, had to be tentatively "yes," for in the absence of such an affirmative answer there would be no need for the research study.

On a more serious plane, he expressed his concern whether data pertaining to segments of conglomerate companies could be reported meaningfully, equitably, and economically. He then went on to note that if the information is to be supplied we have to answer the questions: How much? Where and how should we supply it? And for whom?

He also covered some areas of second-level questions related to definitions of products, entities, organizations, and standard industrial classifications (SIC's), each of which is a possible candidate for the segment for which sales and earnings are to be reported. His tentative conclusions are that no one of the foregoing is universally applicable, and he has suggested that we must leave to the corporations a good degree of flexibility in order to have effective reporting.

I have reviewed some of the conclusions that have emerged from the Financial Research Foundation study, tentative as they are, simply to remind all of us of the character of questions that had to be answered once one started to dig into this subject in depth.

With these sobering conclusions in mind, I shall now enumerate certain provisos I think industry should be granted in making additional disclosure of segments of its business.

First, and foremost, the information so disclosed must be useful and not misleading. This may sound absurdly self-evident, but I don't think this is the case. My concern here is similar to that of Peter Drucker's when he observed that many people believe information consists in pouring out masses of data. As Drucker points out, "this is the one absolutely certain way to deprive people of information." Increased disclosure must not be allowed to fall into the category of data for data's sake.

My second proviso is derived from the fact that this further detailing of information will be based on subjective determinations, which, in turn, would be subject to less stringent audit considerations or even no audit evaluation whatsoever. This occurs because (1) there are no accounting principles to guide us in this area, and (2) the allocation of costs will typically be founded on organization or product lines, depending on management's requirements.

I fear that segmented reporting might come to be treated in the same fashion as the all-inclusive financial statements, which would place upon management the same responsibility—and hence the same legal liability— for segmented statements as those that now exist for all-inclusive statements. Now I do not want to leave the area open for management to willfully provide misleading statements; however, on the other hand, I think we must recognize that by going to this lower level we are getting into an area of much less assuredness regarding the methodology of reporting. Surely, some legal distinction should be made establishing the relative responsibilities of management in providing these two levels of information.

My third proviso is that this segmented information must be provided on the basis the reporting company has chosen, reserving to the reporting company the utmost flexibility of choice. Certainly, the concepts of consistency, materiality, and going concern, which have well defined meanings with respect to the all-inclusive statement, have different meanings when applied to segmented reporting.

In this regard, I am reminded of the speech Duane Orton, chairman of the editorial board of *Think* magazine and director of research for IBM, gave in Montreal at the recent FEI conference. Two of the points he made in his address that dealt with the effects of our rapidly changing business environment on the financial executive, were: (1) to note that the changes have involved a shift from physical to intellectual power, and (2) to predict that this phenomenon would bring about wholesale changes within corporate organizations regarding the relations between superiors and subordinates, line and staff, direct and indirect workers, production and nonproduction workers, and blue collar and white collar workers.

These concepts advanced by Mr. Orton, if true, carry a significant message with respect to those changes we can envision in the future with respect to reporting on segments of the business. These changes, to the extent that cost allocations are based on existing organization, indicate that organization is in for a wholesale shakeup and change; and hence there will be little consistency from period to period in the reporting of product segments.

One example in this area can certainly be drawn from the forecasted change in the definition of what comprises direct as opposed to indirect work. Because direct work in accounting is charged to a particular project, whereas the indirect work must find its way into product cost by some arbitrary method of allocation, any change in work definitions is bound to change direct assignment of cost to an arbitrary assignment of cost, or vice versa.

I understand Dr. Blair's concern over monopolies and combinations that would restrain trade, but it is interesting to note that another point made by Mr. Orton is that technology compounds and concentrates economic power. This is undoubtedly going to provide a continuing backlog of cases for the antitrust department to concern itself with; although, in the context of his remarks, Mr. Orton was expressing his concern for the truly international company's recognizing that their obligations abroad were no different than they were in the United States. In other words, an admonition not to exploit underdeveloped countries.

To return to this matter of subjectivity, I should like to add that whereas I feel people who are calling for this added level of disclosure might be willing to accept subjectivity and might be willing to let the corporations have some flexibility in determining what are the proper segments, I am primarily worried about the future. I recall that we started reporting on an all-inclusive basis with a high amount of flexibility, and then we found a rather clear and pervasive cry for lessening of divergencies.

What will the next request be after we respond to the request for segmented reporting? There might be some merit—although I have expressed many doubts about it—in lessening divergencies of application of accounting principles in the all-inclusive statement, but we are in an entirely different ball park when we talk about segmented reporting. Even Mr. Barr has noted that he feared these things could not be done on a uniform basis as between companies.

Therefore, we are not going to get comparability and we are not going to get standardization, and we should recognize this at the outset. There can be no second step of lessening divergencies in the area of segmented reporting.

My next proviso is that segmented reporting should not result in over-emphasizing the importance of financial statements. I realize that we who are assembled at this symposium are in various shades either oriented to the production of accounting information, the attesting of accounting information, or the use of accounting information. We are all somewhat biased, therefore, in respect to the importance of the accounting product.

If I understand investment circles, however, the current year is regarded as an adequate base for trending future profits—it is, in fact, necessary because companies typically do not forecast the future—but such information is of particular interest to the fundamentalists, who are but one of three types of investors. We also have the Dow-Jones theorists and, lately, the random walkers, to which I would gratuitously include the dart throwers. At least these latter two have a lessened, if not a lack of, interest in the financial statements that we profess to be so concerned about.

Then we have the question of the imperfections of the market place and whether and to what extent financial information controls the market price. As an indication of the areas that are not usually covered in the financial statement, I would point out the necessity of having regard as an investor for the management continuity, the character of management, the company's interest in management development, and the nature of its research and development expenses.

There is also the character of the company's products, how they are received in the market place—and this is something that goes far beyond the mere reporting of sales—and how the company services its products. Actually, there is a whole host of things over which a prospective investor should concern himself that would never become a part of the financial statement.

Further dilution of the importance of segmented financials would seem to be inevitable because this level of reporting would be based on accounting concepts of allocation of costs; however, many managerial decisions are based on concepts of marginal economics, or incremental costs, or on return on investment, the details of which would never be reflected in that form in the segmented reporting now being proposed.

Since I've mentioned return on investment, I should acknowledge that some proponents of segmented reporting want the balance sheet segmented. Cost allocation appears simple compared with the problems of allocating assets and liabilities to segments. And, as Professor Ezra Solomon has noted, there are distinct limitations in the use of such data.

By reason of my position of constantly dealing with investment analysts, as well as being involved in the management of five different investment portfolios, my understanding of where we stand today is that there is no single, organized body of investment theory which, if systematically applied, could cover the transaction costs. If this truly is our situation with respect to investment theory, it raises grave doubts about the efficacy of the projected uses for this additonal disclosure.

This leads me to my next proviso, that segmented reporting should not be allowed to become unduly complex. I am afraid that our present all-inclusive statements have already achieved a degree of complexity that surpasses the comprehension of many small stockholders. To further complicate matters with a new generation of abstruse applications of the accounting art at the segmented level, would not, in my opinion, be a service to many of our investors, nor would it serve to enhance the reliability of investment judgments for investors as a whole.

What could result from this added disclosure, if we do not keep it relatively simple and uncomplicated, is the possibility that the skilled analysts would obtain further advantage over the average stockholder. I have referred to this possibility in past papers and appearances before professional societies as the threat of creating "intellectual insiders." By this, I mean that the skilled analyst might possibly employ this increased disclosure, along with his time for intensive study and research and his access to corporate managers, to gain what, for all practical purposes, would amount to insider information. I do not believe this would be totally pleasing to the gentlemen at the SEC.

Another proviso I would raise is that such increased disclosure should not create kangaroo courts for management trial. Here I am concerned about the effect this disclosure could have on the managerial function. SEC Chairman Manuel Cohen, speaking before the AICPA (American Institute of Certified Public Accountants) last December, expressed the view that increased disclosure, and now I'm quoting, "serves as an important control on corporate managers by requiring them to justify the results of their stewardship," end of quote.

In the business community, this concept has caused some managers to view increased disclosure as a possible means of giving birth to a virulent form of "double management." A recent statement filed with the SEC by the Machinery and Allied Products Institute, for example, said:

> "A real danger in product-line reporting—both to shareholders and, in a larger sense, the economy itself—lies in the possibility of subjecting management to a new volume of criticisms based on limited knowledge and a constricted view of management's problems, plans, and opportunities, which can only tend to reduce management's freedom of action.
>
> "And we must not forget," the statement continues, "that this freedom of capable management to act in the corporation's best overall interests may well be the corporation's principal asset and the thing which gives to the investor's share of ownership its greatest value."

From by own experience with state and federal governments, I have formulated Browne's Law, to wit: "The larger the organization, the more diffused become its objectives." And the corollary to this law is: "The greater the diffusion of objectives, the greater is the tendency to accept mediocre performance."

Decision-making in glass houses, I have observed, where many objectives had to be composed with respect to a great variety of vested interests, seemed designed not to make a worthwhile decision, but, instead, point for a constant deferral of decision and then making the least effective decision in the hope that it would create the least trouble. I would resist the creation of this sort of saddle on management as the result of increased disclosure.

How could this come about?

First of all, this segmented disclosure could lead to a vast number of derivative shareholder suits, the only value of which would be that of nuisance. People who live in glass houses are apt to let nuisances assume far greater importance than they deserve.

I fear this increased disclosure could move us in the direction of examining means, which, in part, is certainly correct since the means should be legal and appropriate, but we should be far more concerned with the ends. Segmented reporting is fraught with the possibility of exposing management to endless discussion and justification of detailed steps, only to hide the end objectives that had been agreed upon.

I am also concerned that this disclosure will bring to the fore the diffusion of objectives that exist between shareholders and management. If this strikes anyone as being paradoxical, I should like to remind you that shareholders do not represent a homogeneous body with uniform objectives. They come to the market as small and large shareholders, as private and institutional holders, as those with short versus long-term interests; and shareholders can be further classified as past, present, and future. Management definitely has a problem in trying to reconcile these disparate objectives among its shareholders.

My final proviso is that this segmented information should be voluntarily disclosed. This is essential because at the level of reporting we are considering there are going to be many instances when this form of disclosure could be tantamount to an invasion of privacy. That this aspect of the subject under discussion has not been given its proper consideration, I would attribute to the growing ambivalence I see in American society and, more particularly, in our government.

At the present time, we are witnessing a resurgence of personal liberty that has had no equal in our history; yet, on the other hand, I observe corporations becoming increasingly hemmed in, harassed, and denied due process of law.

Consider if you will the expansion of civil rights, the rights of dissent, the rights of the accused, and the rights of personal privacy. Hardly a week goes by that there isn't a new decision in our courts that further strengthens the legal rights of the individual. Conversely, hardly a week goes by that some new inroads are not made against the legal rights of corporations. Yet, these encroachments are not protested, deplored, or feared by most Americans.

I shall now quote from the current edition of *American Jurisprudence:*

"So far as property rights are concerned, a private corporation is a 'person' within the meaning of the provisions of the Fifth and Fourteenth Amendments to the Constitution of the United States that no person shall be deprived of life, liberty, or property without due process of law."

This, I believe, indicates that under our laws the legal rights of corporations are not so inferior to human rights as many people are apt to believe. This had led me in past papers to make a rather clear call for the examination as to whether we were not due for the drafting of a Corporate Bill of Rights.

I have made this call because I feel the corporation should not be denied those rights that have been so basic to the economic growth of the American society. In the context of this symposium, I believe corporations should not unwittingly be exposed to their customers or competitors by the forced disclosure of segmented information. It should be possible for such information to be disclosed voluntarily, and in such a manner that all parties will be satisfied, without eroding or destroying the legal rights of the reporting company.

In this regard, I would caution the proponents of product-line reporting to proceed carefully in their efforts. Remember that American business has a spectrum of responsibilities, to its customers, employees, present shareholders, communities, and to society as a whole.

In conclusion, I should like to remind you of my opening position statement. I believe it should be in the corporation's long-run interests to disclose information regarding sales and earnings of segments of the business . . . with certain provisos.

W. D. MACCALLAN

A View from the

Investment Community

I have been asked to discuss the question of product-line reporting from the viewpoint of the financial analyst. Since we have here today able proponents of other perspectives, I intend to interpret this rather narrowly in an attempt to add a little sharpness to the proceedings. In self-defense, however, I must state that even a financial analyst is first of all a citizen and that considerations of the public weal must often take precedence over professional debating points.

I am in favor of product-line reporting. This can hardly be a surprise, since I think this is overwhelmingly the opinion of financial analysts in the investment community. However, I do have a reservation about it that I shall discuss later.

The analyst's job is to build up a picture of the future of a given corporation to which must be attached some measure of the reliability of this projection. If the range of reliability of the estimate can be narrowed, then one can afford to take greater risks on the price of the stock. (This is a particularly important consideration in mature bull markets.) It is towards reducing this range that much of the analyst's effort is devoted, and one of the major factors is the degree of accuracy with which the current position of the company is known. Consider the following example—which is completely mythical but far from inconceivable.

International Black Boxes, Inc. has a marvelous new product, the Mark V, that has a firm position in a new defense contract. The prime contractor is very pleased with it. A new plant has been built. The company reports all this in its annual report, which also shows that earnings are up 30 percent. However, until 3 years ago, this company was known as Schlock Novelties Corp. What is not said in the annual report is that the increase in earnings has derived from sale of 3 million left-over hula hoops to Borneo. The company is actually barely breaking even on the Mark V, since production costs at the new plant are higher than anticipated. As matters stand today the company doesn't have to tell you this. This example should not be dismissed as trivial even though it is at the borderline of credibility. There are managements which would try to avoid an explanation—and would probably succeed as long as new financing, and consequently a prospectus, is unnecessary.

In the actual business world there are many such questions. For instance, how much money was Westinghouse really losing in consumer appliances during the early 1960's? Obviously, the greater the loss the greater the potential improvement in total earnings if this division were to become modestly profitable. There were two factors that made it difficult to come to any highly reliable estimate. First, the Broadcasting Division was and is extremely profitable, particularly on a percentage of sales basis. This, of course, raised overall margins. Second, the lamp bulb operation is a good profit-maker and this unit was included with consumer goods.

Now we're coming down to the first point of contention in product-line reporting, the question of the degree of breakdown. Using Westinghouse as an example, my position is, break out the broadcasting figures and you can marry lamp bulb profits to appliance losses. Expressed like that it sounds like a horse trade. It isn't really though. Common sense will usually provide a quite adequate measure of where the slicing should be performed. There are areas of difficulty, particularly in the petroleum business, which —fortunately for me and for you—I don't feel qualified to discuss. But since I don't want to seem to duck the problem of vertical integration completely, I'll give an example for the chemical industry. Monsanto is a well integrated company in the synthetic fibres area. It makes ammonia and propylene which are converted into acrylonitrile. The latter, aside from being the raw material for acrylic fibre, is also converted, through a unique process, into adiponitrile, the raw material for nylon. I see no reason to break this chain in the reporting process.

However, since this company is set up with a hydrocarbons division, an organic chemicals division and a textiles division, it may be more convenient to break down the figures on divisional lines. This would be equally satisfactory to the analyst.

Such permissiveness may seem contradictory, as if we analysts were desperate for any old bone. In point of fact the major requirement in all financial reporting is consistency. Do it the way you want to do it, but once you've decided on a particular procedure, stick to it. One might well call for a reconciliation any time there was a change of method in breaking down the product line.

The breakdown should not be too fine. While other analysts, particularly those from larger research organizations, may disagree with me, I believe one can be cursed with too much input. My colleagues who interest themselves in the affairs of utilities and railroads seem to have an endless supply of statistics to manipulate but I strongly suspect that 90 percent of them are of very limited value. My own feeling is that any group constituting more than about 15 percent of sales or profits ought to be broken out. A catch-all category to take care of odds and ends is inevitable. The precise method of breakdown, however, I would leave to the individual management's discretion. Corporations have grown up in different ways and you can't carve lamb the way you carve beef. Some discussion has been made of using the SIC classification, but this seems to me to offer grave drawbacks and no advantages.

Please don't misunderstand me about one thing, though. I am not saying that such a breakdown would in any way usher in the millennium, just that it would be helpful and probably adequate. Consider, however, a company that makes nothing but integrated circuits. Here one must know what proportion are resistor-transistor logic, a line that has certainly passed its growth peak and, according to some observers, may start declining in the not too distant future. But this is a specific problem related to a specific company and no reporting requirements can be ideal. All companies present individual problems to the analyst and total comparability is a will-o'-the-wisp.

One authority has raised the interesting suggestion that managements might be tempted to reorganize internally to fit reporting requirements rather than to fulfill the needs of efficient management. This seems to me, per contra, a good argument for leaving management a very broad flexibility here.

The Accounting Principles Board has made a very excellent survey of the problems and the pros and cons of product-line reporting. It's a bit earnest and sometimes fails to distinguish between mountains and molehills, but at least it seems to be objective. It does not, for example, invent problems as some spokesmen appear to do, particularly in discussing the areas of transfer pricing and cost allocation. While I entirely agree that there are thorny points here, there is absolutely no justification (other than sheer obscurantism) for deliberately planting out a hedge of well-fertilized objections. For example, the problem of transfer pricing is something that has been thoroughly explored in tax cases. If the product doesn't have a market price, the profit can be split between divisions on some arbitrary basis. Don't say it can't be done. To worry overmuch about precision suggests one suffers from the delusion that accounting is an exact science. It is only accounting's tool, mathematics, that is exact. And accounting itself is only a tool, both for management and the analyst. While one likes to keep one's tools sharp, and I certainly don't open paint cans with a chisel, you'd be surprised at the uses I find for a linoleum knife.

Stripping the metaphor from my last remark, I'm saying that an analyst regards all figures, even if attested to by the entire Accounting Principles Board, with a good deal of skepticism and certainly as raw material to be manipulated. Thus, going back to my Monsanto example, supposing the company wanted to say it makes a potful of money out of acrylonitrile and very little out of Acrilan, what I would be interested in would be the year to year changes in their profits rather than their absolute levels. The main reason the company makes acrylonitrile is to make synthetic fibres. Economic events that affect one section of the chain must affect the entire chain.

I suppose I have to discuss cost allocation as well. Since I'm not an accountant and barely know a credit from a debit, I shall grant freely that there are all sorts of methods of dealing with headquarters costs and interest charges, to say nothing of research and development expense, and that each method may have something to recommend it, particularly for a given purpose. One of the more persuasive discussions of the difficulties involved is contained in Robert H. Raymond's speech before the Omaha-Lincoln Society of Financial Analysts on May 4, 1967, entitled "Can Conglomerates Be Analyzed?" Mr. Raymond cites an example of a company at whose board meetings where divisional profit statements were presented, such statements were carefully collected afterward. "The reason was not a regard for secrecy, but, instead, a recognition of the fact that these computations were made for the purpose of evaluating management performance. The methods of collection gave consideration to the environment in which each division operated. Without a personal knowledge of that environment, accurate interpretation of the divisional statements would not have been possible."

This statement, while superficially plausible, contains two concealed flaws. First is the assumption that evaluation of management performance is not something of interest outside the board-room. Quite obviously it's something the analyst is doing daily and is a proper matter for his concern. Indeed in some respects it is his ultimate concern. Many companies with extremely undistinguished records have burst into new life after the infusion of more capable management. Second is the flat statement that certain factors are beyond the comprehension of the uninitiated. I have the gravest doubts as to whether, for example, a banker who is on the board of a drug company, attending ten meetings a year, has a better background for evaluating such statements than an analyst who spends one-third or more of his working year studying the drug industry. The outside director is fed additional information that is not available to the analyst no doubt but such information would be completely digestible—indeed palatable—to the analyst.

Perhaps Mr. Raymond did not have the analyst in mind when he wrote this, but was thinking rather of the man in the street or the little old lady in Dubuque. Well, the *New Yorker* magazine is not edited for the latter, but it still has a large circulation. Seriously though, there have been many objections to product-line reporting based on the assertion that such information would tend to confuse rather than to clarify matters. This is a point that seems to me not well taken at all. I doubt if many widows and orphans can read a balance sheet, but that's no reason for not providing it for the benefit of those who can. Today, with the proliferation of mutual funds and the mushrooming of pension funds, there is a progressive professionalization of the management of common stock holdings. More and more the readers of annual reports will tend to be analysts. Surely this should be taken into account.

But to return to the problem of cost allocation, it does not matter to me whether costs are completely distributed or not. It is perfectly satisfactory to have a large lump of unallocated overhead charged at the bottom of the table. Certainly I want the basis to be explained, and certainly I want the method used to be consistent from one accounting period to another. Unquestionably, uniformity of treatment even for those companies in the same line of business is too much to ask for.

In Mr. Raymond's paper which I quoted earlier, he discusses very briefly the concept of direct costing as an approach that might possibly be helpful in this matter. This might be a fruitful suggestion for the experts to follow up although to my untutored eye there must surely be allocation of some costs beyond the purely variable ones.

Turning to a different objection to product-line reporting, we reach the question of whether the revelation of information would give aid and comfort to the competition. While there must be instances where that would be true—for example a company having a division of some importance that makes only one product and is one of the major producers of that item— nevertheless such cases must be very rare. This entire question is used predominantly as a smoke screen and in a manner which tends to do no great credit to the intellectual honesty of the claimant. I think all analysts, in the course of their travels, have from time to time obtained exceedingly useful close estimates of volume, price, costs, and investment from competitors of any given company. It cannot be denied that there are still managements that resent reporting requirements and even attempt to maintain that certain facts are not public when they actually are. This is particularly true of information available from the IOK reports to the SEC or listing statements. I am told that many oil companies are now making IOKs available to analysts on request. My own experience, without having made a statistical analysis, is that the preponderance of companies in other industries would prefer to deny the existence of such documents.

Among the more unusual points raised by opponents of product-line reporting is the question of initial losses in a new business. It has been asked, for example, whether RCA would have been able to make such a large investment in color television if the amount had been made public. Why on earth not? Cabot Corporation has been quite specific about the incredibly long and tedious problems with Cabot Titania. While General Electric remains stoically silent on the dollar cost of its computer problems, Fortune magazine flung some staggering figures about with apparently little effect on the price of the stock. Maybe nobody believes them.

This point was expressed in the APB subcommittee point outline on a somewhat more sophisticated level. It was suggested that potential stockholder criticism of early losses might lead to management's placing an emphasis on short-run results to an extent detrimental to the corporation's long-term welfare. This is nicely phrased, but it implies that managements are singularly pusillanimous. By now, surely, the labor unions would be running such companies. Chairmen are now inured to the annual attacks on charitable donations by a stockholder whom I certainly prefer to leave nameless, and they could probably survive questions on vast development expenditures that do not seem to produce immediate profits. The examples of past fiascos that managements have survived are myriad—Ford's Edsel, Monsanto's Krilium, Nopco's polyurethane venture, Reynolds Tobacco's Tempo, and literally hundreds of consumer products from the giant marketing companies. One must point out, too, that many of these examples are brand names and would thus be part of a larger category for reporting purposes. Mistakes would not be totally exposed.

Even supposing the full story were told, I cannot foresee any very real problem, though there might be some unpleasantness at the annual meeting. If a project fails expensively it does not seem likely that management is laying itself open to any lawsuits, provided such mistakes were honest ones.

If one stretches one's imagination very far indeed, one could conceivably envisage pressure exerted on management by a performance-oriented investor with a large position in the stock. But think how stupid management would be not to resist this pressure. The only weapon such a stockholder has is the threat to sell his stock, and he is obviously going to do that as soon as he has a quick profit. He has no abiding interest in the welfare of the corporation. Hence to give in is only to postpone the use of the weapon; the blow, in itself, is inevitable.

This brings to the surface the possibility that it is not potential stockholder criticism that management is worried about, but the effect of revelation of large losses on the price of the stock. This is a reasonable fear, particularly in view of the current rules on options, but it is one that can be laid at rest. What investors really don't like is a sudden revelation. If you tell them ahead of time that you are planning to put a lot of money into a new project that looks extremely promising but may take some years to work out, they'll usually go along with you. A loss in itself is no barrier to high prices—look at Kalvar or new life insurance companies. In these examples the losses are accepted as necessary forerunners of future profits. Surely by keeping the investment community fully informed, any company, even if it cannot turn a loss into an asset, can persuade the public that it is making a wise investment for the company's future and thus avoid any sudden shocks to the price of its stock.

So far I've spent my time largely in rebuttal although I hope I have, in the process, rendered my own prejudices quite clear. I would, however, like to discuss in greater detail one area where there is certainly a crying need for product-line reporting. I am going to call this area that of the rapidly changing corporation. I am avoiding, for the moment at least, the term "conglomerate," since there appears to be a definitional squabble about it. In an article entitled "The Conglomerate: What is it? Where is it going?," by Chris Welles, published in the June 1967 issue of *The Institutional Investor*, three types of conglomerates are identified. While I would argue with Mr. Welles about his classification of certain companies, the group I am referring to roughly approximates his "Multi-Industry Conglomerates," which he defines as "generally willing to expand into any area that has potential for rapid growth, even if it is totally unrelated to the company's current business." I had thought of calling them "acquisitive companies," but this term seems to have moral overtones that are better excluded.

The problem with these companies is that while there is plenty of material to obtain two-year comparisons on various bases, there are enormous difficulties involved in looking for trends that may be operating over a longer time span. One must recognize to start with that this aspect of analysis is essentially based on attempts to isolate one independent variable and to study its effects on the dependent variable while holding the other independent variables constant. Naturally such attempts are crude, but some facts can be learned. Thus, for a fairly simple steel company the trend of labor costs per ton of steel shipped is obviously meaningful, even though some of the labor costs one is using relate to steel going into inventory rather than steel shipped, and one is also including overhead costs as well. Similarly, for a consumer non-durables company, advertising costs in relation to sales are significant.For a retailer, sales per square foot is a valuable index. But all of these measures contain so many other considerations that their absolute level is questionable. Comparisons between different companies can be exceedingly misleading. For a simple example here, in calculating sales per square foot you may not know for sure whether you're dealing with square feet of selling space or whether you have included off-floor storage in the area. And in considering groceries, sales per linear foot are a better measure anyway. However, the year to year trend in such figures for a given company is highly significant. One can by no means be sure of the meaning of such a trend from the figures alone, but they do point up questions that should be asked. If advertising is rising as a proportion of sales, does this reflect accelerated introduction of new products, or is it merely a defensive action in attempting to hold the market position of an aging product line? If a steel company acquires a department store chain, provided you get a sales breakdown in the following year you may well be able to continue measuring sales per square foot, but you certainly won't be able to look at labor costs per ton of steel. Thus one can assert that cross-industry mergers reduce the effectiveness of the analyst's tools.

With a broadly diversified company, one is reduced to all-encompassing concepts such as operating margins and return on investment. These are still useful series, but there are such a number of independent variables involved that one may be unable to detect significant cross-currents. By looking at the figures for 3M or Kodak you can't see what Xerox did to Thermofax and Verifax. One does note, however, per contra, that the rest of the business of these companies must have been doing better than appears to the naked eye. The eager beaver type of analyst will now assemble trade estimates of Thermofax and Verifax and subtract them out to see what happens. There is a temptation, in the process, to adjust these estimates to leave what looks like a more reasonable remainder. The purpose of this exercise is to consider, assuming total abandonment of these products, whether the companies concerned would be more attractive or less attractive as investments. If you discover a more pronounced growth rate you may well decide the company has a better future after all, even sufficiently so to offset predicted loss of profits as the product is phased out. In which case what you lose in earnings may be outweighed by a prospective increase in the price multiple.

But even such simple measures as operating margins can be massively distorted by repeated acquisitions of large unrelated companies. The following series concerns Gulf & Western Industries, a choice reflecting only the fact that it is the company of this type with which I am most familiar. Let us investigate the behavior of pre-tax profit margins over the last 5 years. Unfortunately results for the year to July 31, 1967, were not available when this table was developed.

GULF & WESTERN INDUSTRIES

Year to 7/31	$ Millions				
	1966	1965	1964	1963	1962
Sales—original report	317.5	182.1	117.2	92.5	65.6
adjusted following year		277.2	129.6	107.2	71.4
Pre-tax Net—original report	30.1	10.0	6.0	5.2	3.3
adjusted following year		22.8	7.2	5.7	4.0
Pre-tax Profit Margin—original report	9.5%	5.5%	5.1%	5.6%	5.0%
adjusted following year		8.2	5.5	5.3	5.6

The adjustments in the following year represent acquisitions by pooling. Unfortunately in fiscal 1966 Gulf & Western acquired New Jersey Zinc on a partly pooled basis, and the adjustment for 1965 reflects only that part of the business acquired on a pooled basis. For the benefit of those unfamiliar with this occurrence I should explain that Gulf & Western bought some of the New Jersey Zinc stock for cash and subsequently made an exchange of stock offer for the balance. Only that portion acquired by exchange of stock is pooled. This may make some sort of sense to accountants and the IRS, but it is sheer nonsense from any common sense point of view.

The cash purchase preceded the exchange offer and was the basis for it. The concept of, for comparative purposes, owning part of a company is utterly absurd. I do understand why it is done, but the mind boggles and the throat gags. The problem involves, of course, how you would otherwise develop earnings per share. Possibly you could pro forma the acquired company on the basis of retroactively shrinking its capitalization to the extent shares were purchased for cash. I really don't know the answer, but the present theory of pooling has been elaborated exactly as the epicyclic theory of Ptolemy concerning the motion of the heavenly bodies was elaborated. Anything so complicated cannot possibly be right.

But to get back to my table, one observes that pre-tax margins were in the 5–5½ percent area until the acquisition of New Jersey Zinc when they almost doubled, and that, except for 1963, the acquisitions have tended to raise margins. This is hardly very illuminating. What has been the experience in the margins of companies acquired several years ago since they have been taken into the fold? Deponent sayeth not. This is a vital consideration because one wishes to know whether acquired companies are just gobbled up for their short-term effect on earnings or whether they are coddled and cossetted until they start growing faster and more profitably.

Of course it can be argued that with such companies margins on sales are neither here nor there. Some lines produce more and some less. One must consider the return on investment. This is, as far as it goes, an apt observation, since this criterion is a cardinal one used in operating such a company. But again we run into pitfalls. To start with, we must agree to ignore the retroactive effect of poolings, since we are interested in what has been done for the stockholder through a combination of acquisitions and operating expertise. Obviously this leads to a use of average investment or else the simple fact of a large acquisition would blow up the subsequent year's return on investment. Ideally the average should be based on the ratio of the proportion of the fiscal year for which the acquisition was effective, but let's assume we're too lazy. That gives us, crudely, a denominator. How about the numerator? Here we are faced with an insoluble problem since we are given pooled figures, as if the acquisition had been in effect all year. But it wasn't. So again the resultant ratio would be overstated. There is just no point in making any such calculation.

What, then, is the poor benighted analyst to do? He can make two-year comparisons for any pair of consecutive years that have a certain amount of reliability. Beyond that, he is, as far as conventional financial reporting is concerned, at a loss. Fortunately, in the present instance, Gulf & Western on page 7 of their 1966 annual report gives a most unusual and interesting table from which one can get considerable insight into the internal growth of acquired companies subsequent to their acquisition. All companies acquired in any one year are considered as a unit, and the percentage increase in sales and profits of each annual unit is given up to the date of the report. The equivalent compound annual rate of increase is also given. While more sophisticated interpretations are, I suppose, possible, I read the table simply as showing that the acquisitions have continued to show substantial growth since they were acquired.

This is extremely useful information but does not particularly assist in the construction of projections. One simply must go back to the individual segments of the corporation, make separate projections for each, and add them up. To date this has not been an impossible task, since the major acquisitions have been recent enough for the last available statements of these companies as independent entities to retain some pertinence. One does know what has been going on in the zinc market and there is plenty of history to guide one towards the likely effects on New Jersey Zinc's operations. But as time goes on and the influence of new management begins to take hold, such methods are likely to become less and less valid unless one can really keep up with changes that new management is making. Furthermore, the acquisition of Paramount Pictures introduces a major new variable into the prospects for corporate profits. Since the new accounting rules insist on rental agreements with television networks being taken into profit at the time the contracts are written, we are faced with a completely unpredictable element in earnings. For the year to July 31, 1967, Gulf & Western will earn in the area of $40 million after preferred dividends. Rental agreements for feature films have recently been running about $500,000 per film and virtually all cost elements have already been written off. Thus, rental agreements for as few as eight feature films come close to 10 percent of the whole company's net available for common. Unless product-line reporting is available, such influences, the timing of which must tend to be erratic, will be unidentifiable, and although detailed narrative in the annual report may go far towards explaining what actually happened, nothing can quite replace the actual figures.

If I appear to have been taking Gulf & Western to task, I hasten to repeat that this company was used merely as a convenient illustration. I am in no manner criticizing that management's forthrightness in discussing the company.

This brings me conveniently to the area of reservation about product-line reporting that I mentioned at the start of my talk. The illustration I have just been using is one of a complex situation which demands a good deal of effort to grasp properly. It is not, at present, an impossible task, but it is one that a number of people will shy away from. This creates the possibility of an investment opportunity that is being overlooked. And this kind of area is one that I mine for my livelihood. In a pure investment situation, if one party has made a good buy, the other has made a bad sale. If each party had the same information and if that information were complete, such a situation could not logically exist. While such an era would see me on the street selling apples, it seems hardly likely to be brought to birth by product-line reporting.

ROBERT E. PFENNING

A View from the

Investment Community–

Comments

As the introduction has indicated, virtually all of my business career has been spent in the employ of General Electric Company, and most of that time I have been working in the accounting and financial area. Early in that experience I learned that General Electric Company was sincerely interested in reporting meaningful information to its owners and to prospective owners. During the time I have been in a position to have some influence on the Company's reporting of the results of its operations, I have tried to follow the path of my predecessors, and my associates in the Executive Office have shared my interest in better reporting. Over the years we have made significant improvements in our reporting, and we keep working at it. Accordingly, it was very encouraging to all of us in General Electric when early this year we received a citation from The Financial Analysts Federation for "Excellence in Corporate Reporting for the Year 1965 as judged by the standards of professional financial analysts."

Because of my long-standing sincere interest in better corporate reporting, I have been disturbed and frustrated by the great debate which has been raging for over two years and in which we are participating here today. What bothers me most is that this great debate masquerades as a discussion of the necessary, most logical, next-big-step in improvement of corporate reporting. Actually, it has degenerated into an enumeration by certain groups of people of the dangers and difficulties they see in attempting product-line reporting of profitability and then a rebuttal by other groups that such dangers and difficulties don't exist. Very little attention is being paid to determining legitimate needs of the investing public and what should be done to meet them. This frustrating and futile process began when the desirability of product-line profitability reporting was espoused in an antitrust context and the espousal included the suggestion that additional laws might be required to obtain the information thought desirable for antitrust investigative purposes. The Securities and Exchange Commission very correctly pointed out that additional laws were not necessary to obtain such information if it were deemed desirable to have it for the use and protection of the investing public. And then others got in the act with the thesis that protection of the investing public required reporting of product-line profitability.

I am sure Mr. MacCallan would agree that he and his associates who serve the investing public are eager to receive meaningful information which will help them provide their services. He might even agree that in the absence of meaningful information, they are eager to receive *any* information which somehow might prove to be useful to them. I suggest that perhaps some of his associates were motivated primarily by this latter desire in jumping on the band-wagon for product-line profitability reporting. I say this because I have listened and read and waited for a clear delineation of the real informational needs of the investing public together with a sound analysis of what kinds of information might best fill those needs. What I have been hearing are listings of informational needs, to be sure, but with only the allegation or assumption that reporting of profits by product lines would be helpful in meeting the needs enumerated. I have heard very little about other types of information which would be even more helpful.

When I was asked to participate in this symposium, I was attracted by the fact that the word "need" appeared in the program several times. I was particularly hopeful that the paper dealing with the viewpoint of the investment community, on which my discussion was to be based, would shed some light on the real needs of investors and how corporations could best meet those needs. However, in the first part of his paper, Mr. MacCallan has chosen to rebut the opinions of those who over the last two years have tried to set forth the difficulties which would be involved if a large, diversified, integrated company were required to report profits by product line and the ways in which this information might be more misleading than helpful. It seems to me that we ought to try to find better use for our time than having me rebut the rebuttal. I would like to mention, however, that the problems and difficulties which Mr. MacCallan rather casually dismisses are real and not imaginary. Those of us who are charged with the responsibility of reporting meaningful information to the management and directors of our companies have learned a long time ago that it is impossible to obtain the same degree of accuracy and reasonableness in the segmentation of a company's profitability as is attained in reporting the company's total results. We also have learned another extremely important fact that is entirely disregarded in most discussions of reporting of segmented profitability. This fact is that in a large, diversified, integrated company, the most meaningful way to report a segmentation of the company's profitability is a segregation based on the assignment to managers and organization components of the responsibility for producing the profit. Whether or not this results in a segmentation according to product lines is of course entirely dependent upon the internal organization of the company and the nature of the assignment of responsibility for the various areas of its operations. This assignment of responsibility may or may not be according to product lines, industry classifications, or any of the other bases which have been suggested for the public reporting of a company's profitability. Because of this situation, it is entirely inappropriate to confine discussion to the needs, desirability, or problems associated with reporting profitability by product line. I am sure that most large, diversified, integrated companies would be unable to do that kind of reporting without either abandoning what they have felt was desirable for management purposes or incurring thousands of dollars of additional costs to accumulate information on a second basis for external reporting purposes. On the other hand, if the internal reporting on a responsibility basis were to be made public, it would be either unacceptable or misleading for a number of reasons, not the least of which is the inconsistencies from year to year which result from the many reassignments of responsibilities which occur in any dynamic organization.

At this point I want to state as clearly as I can that I am in favor of disclosing meaningful operating information which will help to explain the *reasons* behind a company's profitability and particularly the changes in that profitability from one reporting period to another. I am opposed to external reporting of results of operations on any segmented basis because I know that this will not supply *reasons* but only more voluminous and perhaps misleading information. In his example of International Black Boxes, Inc., Mr. MacCallan intimated that a segregation of profits between the Mark V line and the hula hoop product line would have solved the information problems with respect to the Company's 30 percent improvement in earnings. He tells us that the real reason was the sale of 3 million left-over hula hoops to Borneo. This is the information which should have been disclosed by the Company. The only contribution from reporting of profitability by product lines in this instance would have been that it would have given Mr. MacCallan the opportunity to ask specific questions as to what happened in the hula hoop product line. However, in my opinion, the answer should have been furnished by the Company in the first place. My point is that the reporting of profits by product line will not in and of itself supply the information which is really needed by the investor. Let me make this point again with respect to another one of Mr. MacCallan's examples. He refers to a company that makes nothing but integrated circuits and points out that it is important for him to know what proportion of these circuits embody resistor-transistor logic because this particular line has passed its growth peak and, according to some observers, may start declining. I submit that what Mr. MacCallan really needs in order to get this information is a segregation of the sales of this company, together with some indication of where they are channeling their efforts in integrated circuits for the future. It is this type of reference to information needs with the intimation that reporting of profits by product line will supply the needs, when in fact it won't, that has made this whole great debate extremely frustrating to those who are sincerely interested in supplying the legitimate information needs of investors. Somehow I get the feeling I am watching great efforts to draw a precise line from an unwarranted assumption to a foregone conclusion. If I do nothing else today, I want to leave with you the plea that we divert some of our efforts from the clamor for and resistance to reporting of profits by product line and direct them to determination of legitimate investor information needs and just what kind of information would be most helpful in meeting those needs.

Professor Mautz published a conceptual article in the July issue of *Financial Executive*. In this article he identified three investment variables concerning which investors need information. He went on to say:

> "If a separable component of a company has experience significantly different from other identifiable components in one or more of *the three investment variables*, an investor might well be interested. If Division A is much riskier than Division B, if Product A has a much greater potential for growth than Product B, if Market A is highly resistant to economic fluctuations while Market B is not, an investor might be influenced to make decisions he would not make if he felt that throughout the company there was but a single, uniform, indivisible rate of risk, the same indivisible potential for growth, the same indivisible resistance of susceptibility to economic fluctuation and other hazards."

Frankly, I don't see how knowing the *profits* of Division A and B separately will help very much in reaching a conclusion on whether the business of Division A is riskier than B, or the products in Division A have potential for greater growth than those in B, or the market served by Division A is more resistant to economic fluctuations than the market served by B. Some other information is required to reach these conclusions. Also some other information is required to meet another investor concern which has been identified by Professor Mautz as being the concern "about the calibre of management."

I repeat that it would have been more helpful to the cause of better corporate reporting if all of us had devoted our efforts to the determination of legitimate investor information needs and just what kind of information would be most helpful in meeting those needs.

The latter part of Mr. MacCallan's paper was devoted to the difficulties encountered by a financial analyst in forecasting future profitability of a rapidly changing corporation. The paper then ends on a light note when Mr. MacCallan points out that having complete information in the hands of all investors or prospective investors could lead to simultaneous consistent buy or sell decisions and hence the elimination of security transactions, markets, and his job. He does not see this horrible state of affairs resulting from the reporting of profitability by product lines. I would like to add that I doubt that it will ever come about no matter how much information is reported. Investment decisions will always require the application of judgment to whatever information is available. As Mr. MacCallan points out, the analyst is deeply involved in supplying some of this judgment, a large part of which involves forecasting future events. As a matter of fact, this forecasting activity is fast becoming a matter of great concern to those of us who have responsibility for reporting corporate results of operations.

In a speech made earlier this year before the Economic Club of Detroit, David L. Babson discussed some new factors and forces in the investment field. His remarks included the following:

> "The growing army of security analysts is another major development. There are almost 10,000 of them compared with 1600 in 1948 and probably 100 in 1932. We now have 8 analysts per listed company versus 3 in 1952 and perhaps one at the end of the war. Their news and rumors spread like wildfire from coast to coast with an almost instantaneous effect on prices. Their reports of companies with 'good stories' are repeated and distributed by others within a matter of hours. Earnings statements these days are judged, not on whether they are good or poor, but whether they are better or worse than the analysts have been estimating."

We accountants in industry are well aware of our limitations as historians in accurately recording and reporting results of operations, but we also know that we are far better historians than we are prophets. I firmly believe that corporate reporting of profitability should be based on what *has* happened and not what *might* happen. However, I well appreciate that good historical reporting will help those who wish to prophesy the future. The question then resolves itself again to a definition of legitimate needs and how can those needs be met. If the need is for labor costs per ton of steel, advertising costs in relation to sales, or sales per square foot, then the furnishing of profitability by product lines will not meet the needs. Neither will segmented profitability reporting provide the *reason* for the changes in a changing corporation's profits, whether it changes by reason of internal growth or by merger or acquisition. If the changes are significant, the reasons should be furnished by the corporation voluntarily. I admit there is a great deal of opportunity for improvement in reporting such reasons just as there is a need for improvement in reporting results of mergers and acquisitions, as Mr. MacCallan points out. Segmented profitability reporting will not provide that improvement, however, and it seems to me that we should spend our time in determining what will best serve the investing public rather than debating the efficacy of product-line profitability reporting.

Because of the importance of judgment in investment decisions and the fact that this judgment is more and more being supplied by professional financial analysts, I would like to close on the same light note as Mr. Mac-Callan but with a suggestion for a means for providing additional protection to the investing public. I might add that the desirable situation which would transpire from the adoption of my suggestion has no more chance of being created than the situation which Mr. MacCallan imagined in his closing remarks. I suggest that any individual or firm which makes public an analysis of any corporation whose securities are listed on a stock exchange be required to file a copy of this analysis with the Securities and Exchange Commission. Of course, the form and content of the filing would be as prescribed by the Commission. At the end of each year the Commission would summarize the filings made during the previous three years and this summary would be published, showing separately of course, the prophecies made by each analyst. This publication would become an integral part of all statements of a corporation filed with the Commission. Any interested person, therefore, would have in one place complete information on the results of operations of the corporation and a basis for evaluating the judgment of the various analysts who had forecast those results. This suggestion is made entirely in the interests of having more complete information in the hands of investors and potential investors and not for the purpose of placing any particular analyst or analysts on the street selling apples.

JOHN J. HARTMANN

A View

from Management

In calling this a view from management I use the word view in the sense of scene rather than in the sense of opinion. The scene reported upon is the arena in which one's theories become practices. It is a very specific and somewhat personal view, because it is the story of just one company, the pressures faced by that company, the environment in which that company operated and its responses to that environment, all with respect to its financial reporting posture.

Before discussing that company, Kern County Land Company, I should like to comment upon a major point of terminology. We use the expression "product-line profit reporting by conglomerate corporations." I don't think we really mean all that that expression suggests. It seems to me that our focus is on the loss of financial information suffered by outsiders when a business enterprise becomes a part of that strange thing called a "conglomerate." When this occurs no one loses "product-line" profit analysis because such disclosure has never been a generally accepted practice of American business. What is lost is "industry source" data and this is what is needed by an outsider attempting to analyze a conglomerate enterprise. An example—when J. I. Case Company, a maker of agricultural and construction equipment, became a part of Kern County Land Company, a conglomerate, the data that was subject to disappearance was not Case's profits on tractors versus combines, but the share of Kern's earnings attributable to the industry of which Case is a part.

For its external reporting Kern County Land has never gone as far as "product-line profit reporting"—it has been in the forefront of disclosure by going as far as "profit by industry." It is about this concept that I shall speak.

To understand the financial reporting of Kern County Land Company, we have to go back to its beginnings. We also have to go to its endings so that we will know what some of the things were that happened to that company, and why we will never know what the ultimate results of its disclosure policies might have been.

Kern County Land Company's beginnings were in California, late in the last century. It was founded by two gentlemen whose names are prominent in the California history of that time—Lloyd Tevis and James Ben Ali Haggin, and a third man, by the name of Carr, who disappears from the record early in the story. At first, the company was dedicated to land acquisition, development, and sale, and farming and cattle raising in the southern end of the San Joaquin Valley in California and on desert ranches in Arizona and New Mexico. In 1903, revenues first began to flow from oil properties. These revenues were very modest until the year 1936 when Shell Oil Company, through the use of then new exploration techniques discovered the Ten-Section oil field on the company's properties in California. In the immediately following years several other giant oil fields were discovered on company lands in the same area.

Year-end 1956 can be taken as a point of change in the nature of Kern County Land Company. By 1956, net operating revenues of $19 million from oil royalties represented by far the major source of corporate income. A modest oil exploration program had been undertaken and was approaching profitability. The flow of oil royalties had been used to develop farming lands of the company, and to expand its cattle operations, which together by 1956 were providing about $1 million of operating income. At that time, the company owned approximately two million acres of land in California Arizona, New Mexico, and Oregon. The California properties were (and are) centered about Bakersfield some 300 miles south of San Francisco and 100 miles north of Los Angeles. This was a company well known to, and well thought of by, the investing public. In the years following 1956 came dramatic change.

Late in the year 1957, the company joined with two young engineers in the formation of Watkins-Johnson Company, to engage in the manufacture of electron devices. Watkins-Johnson is now a leader in its field in design, development, and production of traveling wave tubes, backward wave oscillators, YIG filters, and other devices. At mid-1959, Walker Manufacturing Company, a manufacturer of automotive exhaust systems and other automobile parts, was acquired through an exchange of stock. Walker, while its name is not well known, provides more than 10 percent of all of the exhaust systems used by the original equipment automobile manufacturers in America and about 25 percent of the systems sold in the aftermarket. In 1964, Kern County Land Company acquired, for cash, a controlling interest in J. I. Case Company, a major manufacturer of agricultural tractors and other agricultural equipment, and of backhoes, loaders and similar items for use by the construction industry. Case is one of the major producers of these sorts of equipment. At this point in time, the company had changed basically from its original form. It had, through its entry in the years following 1956 into manufacturing activities, materially changed the nature of its operations. It had moved from its early pastoral nature to become a major industrial complex. It was no longer the typical land-oil royalty company, but something very different. What it was was hard to understand. It was referred to, in writing, as a "strange contraption." The investing public no longer knew how to classify it.

Let us now turn to the financial reporting of Kern County Land Company. As you would expect, the internal financial reporting of the company had changed very greatly over the years, following very closely in its major outlines the evolving organizational structure. The major categorization was thus by industry association. As you would expect, great detail was available within these major categories concerning results by product line and individual items within each line. Also, as you would expect, this latter analysis seldom went beyond gross profit. The major category analysis was carried to a net earnings figure after overhead and tax on that particular block of activities.

Meanwhile, the external reporting had, as it became more complex, become more summarized. While the first published reports of the company, after it became publicly owned, showed considerable detail by major activity, by 1963 this had disappeared.

Within the company we were coming to agreement that, in some form, additional disclosure was appropriate. We felt the matter was a serious one and, in our discussions, three main arguments were made against added disclosure.

The first was based on competitive considerations. It was feared, particularly with respect to our auto parts operations, that display of detailed financial results would work to our competitive disadvantage.

The second argument was philosophical and framed as follows. The shareowner should look to the management for operation of the aggregate assets of the venture, and should judge that management on the single result of that aggregate operation. It is difficult to identify all the trade-offs that have taken place in arriving at this single result, and it is imprudent to isolate operational areas for individual evaluation without being in possession of all of the relevant trade-off data.

The third argument is a very practical one that all corporate financial officers face concerning detailed disclosure of financial affairs, and it arises from the problem of ambiguity. We are quite willing to live with ambiguous financial data within our corporation where we have the opportunity for extensive and intensive explanations, and where the people using the data are familiar not only with its content, but with its limitations. When we go to the outside, we feel that the information should stand on its own and be clear of itself. It is the very nature of business today that only the most gross numbers are susceptible to this degree of definition.

As we prepared to issue the 1964 Annual Report to shareowners, those arguing for added disclosure held the day, but before going on to a report of the action we took let us divert a moment to the problem of external dissatisfaction with our reporting. As I mentioned earlier, we had become difficult to understand, not only to our shareowners but also to the investing public in general and its interpreters, the security analysts.

The attitude of the analysts is particularly pertinent. They virtually demanded that we give them information concerning our earnings by operation, even though we were not making general disclosure of this fact. We steadfastly refused to give to them anything that we were not generally releasing. Lack of information begot lack of understanding, and, eventually, this lack of understanding began to be reflected in some lack of interest. A few analysts expressed the view that they could more productively spend their time keeping track of companies which they could better understand and more safely interpret. The funds began to have smaller and smaller investments in our stock and our price earnings ratio began to decline from its historic levels. I do not know whether there were direct cause and effect relations in this series of developments.

To talk now of our response to the problem, we had considered providing some sort of supplemental, interpretive reports for analysts' use, but felt that unless we could really integrate more successful reporting into our official reports, we hadn't done the job. By year-end 1964, we were finally convinced that profit reporting by major activity was appropriate to Kern County Land Company. At that time, J. I. Case and Watkins-Johnson, the latter of which had grown to significant proportions in our income statement, were issuing Annual Reports to their minority shareowners. In our Annual Report for the year 1964, as supplemental information in tabular form, we presented an analysis of our earnings by major operational segment on a net after-tax basis. It is worth stressing here that until income reporting for a conglomerate permits some sort of product-line or industry source analysis of the bottom line figure that the job has not been finished. Disclosure of revenue source is less than half the job. The impact of industry variations in gross profit ratios, capital costs, and tax rates can obscure or even invalidate interpretations of the meaning for the company of gross revenue trends. We chose not to allocate general corporate overhead, nor did we correct for leverage differences and interest costs as between the various groups. As a result of these decisions, it might not be precisely meaningful to compare our results by segment with comparable other operations outside Kern County Land Company, but these reporting techniques did yield year-to-year conformity, which provided profit source trend data. And, of course, the data were generally reliable indicators of our results in a given industry.

In our reports for the years 1965 and 1966, these breakdowns were expanded going into subsegments of our operations. At the same time, in the narrative section of the report, we commented upon gross revenues by operation. As I have said, the results of both J. I. Case and Watkins-Johnson were available separately in detail.

Within the interpretive limitations I have mentioned, we were quite satisfied with the results of the improvement in our income reporting.

We did not undertake this amplified reporting step lightly. It was our responsibility to assure, to the extent possible, that our readers truly comprehended the material provided. This was a complex assignment primarily because of the ambiguity problem mentioned before. The usual financial reporting exists in the sea of "generally accepted accounting principles," which provide a vast, if implicit, set of definitions and explanatory and limiting footnotes to the statements. The final net earnings figure to which our source analysis footed was computed in accordance with generally accepted accounting principles. Our readers knew this and could rely upon it for it was the same figure that appeared in our certified statements. Concerning the analysis itself they had no such assurance. The analysis was not covered by our accountants' certificate nor identified with the other financial data nor subjected to the financial notes. Finally, we provided nothing editorially by way of explanation as to underlying principles. The readers had to accept that the presentation was somehow "fair" and "consistent" and for this they had to rely somehow on the good name of the company and its management. They had one element of external protection, in that I am quite sure that our public accountants would withhold their certificate from any report which contained any statement within the field of their expertise which in their judgment had the effect of misleading the reader.

We were in the position of accepting this responsibility without any real frame of reference to guide us. Internal accounting principles are those which work for that particular company. There is no need for them to ever have been accepted by anyone else nor need they be consistent company-wide nor from period to period.

To what standards had we implicity subscribed? It seems to me that the reader was certainly entitled to assume that at least three principles were being followed.

1. In no way was income being arbitrarily shifted from one category to another.
2. The presentation was consistent for the periods shown.
3. "Generally accepted accounting principles" were at least in a broad way being applied.

Our internal systems gave us no real problem with respect to these standards. However, the basic reliance of the reader, under the circumstances, had to be on the good faith, good judgment, and professionalism of those creating the statement.

Before leaving this particular point I should like to raise a question.

In view of the hazards inherent in the present unstructured situation, should companies be precluded from any income breakdown pending development of some code, or set of guidelines, or body of principles? We have all been appalled, if enthralled, recently by disclosures under SEC and Court inquiry into the financial reporting practices of certain companies. What is your reaction to the thought of such a company "amplifying" its financials as it saw fit without any frame of reference or audit?

To turn to results, I can report these results observed since the appearance of our detailed income statements. Security analysts were more interested in our company as a result of the added information available to them, and I feel they understood our situation much better than they had in the past. It is interesting that their visits were not as numerous, nor as lengthy, as they had been in the past. We were providing them, in writing, with most of the information that they wanted, and their visits thus became for the most part general discussions about the future of the company. It made our life easier, because we were willing to tell people almost more than they really wanted to know. We were not faced with the problem of trying to hew to a very narrow line of disclosure. I can't deny that, at times, there were embarrassing questions asked as a result of our disclosure practices. In our most recent Annual Report, you will see bracketed figures in the operational summaries. These focused attention of the shareowners and the analysts upon problem operations. We have to acknowledge, however, that this is probably where their attention should be focused, just as management's certainly should be. We felt that people were entitled to ask questions about those operations that appeared to be in trouble, and that we should be in a position to answer them. We did not feel it proper to conceal problems of that sort in aggregate numbers.

I will never be able to report to you any long-range results of our decision. In early May of this year a tender offer was made for the stock of Kern County Land Company at a price about a third above the market. Within a period of a few days, this offer had resulted in the accumulation of about 20 percent of the stock of the company in the hands of one shareowner. The offer was opposed by the Directors of Kern County Land Company as being not in the best interests of the shareowners. In mid-May, the Board approved a plan of merger with Tenneco Inc., subject to the approval of the shareowners. In July, at a special meeting of the shareowners, this plan was, by a vast majority, approved, and at the end of August, the transaction was closed. As a result, Kern County Land Company is now a wholly owned subsidiary of Tenneco Inc., and its separate financial reports will no longer appear. The interests of our 20,000 shareowners are now served by their holding of stock in Tenneco, and investment decisions, with respect to that stock, will be based upon the financial reports of Tenneco.

This recent change in the fortunes of our company means that we will never know whether our change in disclosure practice was successful in telling our story to the investing public in a way that would give them confidence in our stock. We will never know whether our price earnings ratio would return to its former levels.

That is the end of the story. As I warned you, this has been a personal and a narrow view of the question we are discussing—I hope it has been of interest.

C. REED PARKER

A View

from Management—

Comments

In the midst of the rapidly proliferating material on reporting a breakdown of profits by conglomerate corporations, Mr. Hartmann's comments seem all but unique. Here is actual testimony from a party at interest—an officer of a conglomerate company talking about his company's experience with the fact of profit breakdown reporting—rather than theorizing about or advocacy pro or con such reporting.

As testimony concerning facts, Mr. Hartmann's words do not lend themselves to the kind of analysis that runs, "His reasoning in this regard seems faulty because . . ." or, "His conclusion here is excellent because. . . ." However, as an investment analyst, I was particularly impressed by several of his statements. I would like to repeat them and to add comments from my own experience and from that of my firm.

First, and perhaps most important, was the statement of what Kern County Land's earnings breakdown did and did not provide: "We chose not to allocate general corporate overhead, nor did we attempt to correct for leverage differences and interest costs as between the various groups. As a result of these decisions, it would not be precisely meaningful to compare our results by segment with comparable other operations outside Kern County Land Company, but these reporting techniques did yield year-to-year conformity, which provided profit source trend data."

In my opinion, profit breakdown reporting is quite unlikely ever to provide the investment analyst with meaningful comparisons of results of a segment of company X against results of a similar segment of company Y. In the first place, the business of different companies within a given industry, no matter how narrowly defined, is never exactly identical. One company's line of toiletries or passenger cars or steels is inevitably going to be broader than those of another company. Quite likely each company produces some items that the other does not.

Further, the markets for similar products are unlikely to provide the

71

same mix from one company to another. Standard Brands sells a significantly larger proportion of its Chase & Sanborn coffee to institutions than does General Foods of its Maxwell House. General Tire sells a much smaller proportion of its tires as original equipment than does Uniroyal. Quite likely, no other muffler manufacturer has the same proportions going to original equipment and after markets as Kern County's Walker Manufacturing.

Secondly, most industries are not susceptible of narrow definition. Chemicals to Warner-Lambert are quite sophisticated pharmaceutical raw materials, while to Kaiser Aluminum a most important chemical is nitrogen for agricultural fertilizers, and for National Lead it is titanium dioxide. Thus, the same "product lines" for different companies involve significant variance in the key investment oriented measures of profitability, risk, and growth potential. And this comes from differences in the products themselves and their markets, long before one meets the problems of intracompany pricing and proper allocation of centralized research, general and administrative expenses, capital costs, and the like.

But this is no argument against the utility, for investment analytical purposes, of a breakdown of profit by industry. In my firm's work of developing investment research material for professional investors we become more impressed each day with the importance of considering each company as a unique entity. Down through the fundamentals of products, markets, and especially in the key qualitative area of management prowess, fewer and fewer companies have close comparisons. Only when one comes toward the end of the analytic trail and has returned to aggregate valuations of profitability, risk, and growth potential is the analyst ready to compare company with company, specific investment security with specific investment security.

The importance of a profit breakdown by industry is to give the investor just what Mr. Hartmann states his figures did—"year-to-year conformity, which provided profit source trend data" for the company in question. And, since year-to-year conformity in providing profit source trend data is what seems likely to be of most utility to the investor, it would appear to follow that the methodology used to provide it need not—and perhaps cannot or at least should not—be rigidly prescribed. For some companies it may be meaningful to allocate all costs and to develop after-tax net earning figures for each industry. But, I can easily conceive that for others the most meaningful profit source trend data would come from some defined profit level up one or more levels from the bottom of the income statement.

In brief, my opinion would be that investors would be best served by a profit breakdown tailored to fit the company in question rather than one conformed to some set of standards applicable to all companies. Mr. Hartmann has most appropriately raised the issue of who is to determine this fit—that is to determine the type of profit breakdown most meaningful to the investor for a given company. I do not now see any better allocation of responsibility than that followed by Kern County—with management assuming primary responsibility and the public accounting firm auditor being essentially a consultant within the area of its expertise. In any case, following the three principles listed by Mr. Hartmann—no arbitrary shifting of profit from one category to another, consistency for the periods shown, and application in at least a broad way of "generally accepted accounting principles"—seems adequate to protect the investor's interest and to provide him with meaningful data.

Another of Mr. Hartmann's key statements concerned the effect of disclosing unfavorable results for one or more segments of profit as he said: "I can't deny that, at times, there were embarrassing questions asked as a result of our disclosure practices. In our most recent Annual Report, you will see bracketed figures in the operational summaries. These focused attention of the shareowners and the analysts upon problem operations. We have to acknowledge, however, that this is probably where their attention should be focused, just as management's certainly should be."

It has been argued that managements will be less willing to risk large sums in developing new products or markets if the cost involved must be publicly recorded each year. I do not feel naive in arguing that it is precisely in the area of loss operations that profit by industry reporting would provide management with a highly useful tool in providing investors with a more accurate understanding of a company's potential. Deere & Company common presently sells at a significantly higher valuation of 1967 earnings than does its principal farm equipment competitor, International Harvester. I know that guessing why one company has a higher price earnings ratio than another is exactly that—guessing. However, I suspect that a principal reason in this case is knowledge by investors that Deere is currently sustaining a relatively enormous loss in its foreign operations plus acceptance of management's argument that this loss is susceptible of eventual replacement by a reasonable rate of profit.

I also suspect that a company such as RCA could have made it possible for investors to value its common stock higher in the early years of color TV if it had revealed the size of manufacturing and telecasting losses applicable to color. Suppose an investor (or his analyst adviser)—having only RCA's composite earnings figure and an interpretive statement in the annual report that color television activities were in the red—had estimated that the level of the current loss was, let us say, minus five units, and that profit potential within a few years was, let us say, plus one hundred units. Had he known that the present base was in fact a much larger loss than he had guessed—twenty-five units—the investor could well have concluded that the growth potential for RCA's color television business was correspondingly larger than he had anticipated—that is from minus twenty-five to plus one hundred rather than from minus five to plus one hundred. Moreover, the investor would simultaneously have learned that in fact some other segments of RCA's business had higher levels of profitability than he had estimated. Both of these factors could well have influenced the investor to have a higher regard for RCA common than he had from analyzing only composite earnings figures enhanced only by a relatively unspecific interpretive comment.

It may well be that for some companies revelation of profit by industry data would result in lower market valuations for their securities and penalties as regards cost of new capital. But, this lower market valuation would be justified, I believe, by a clearer understanding on the part of investors (via more facts and management's best effort to interpret those facts) of the profitability, risk, and growth potential of the company in question. If so, one need not be an investor to argue in favor of profit by industry reporting in such cases. Rather one need merely be a believer in the free enterprise system with its axioms of answerability of management to the company's shareholder owners and of sensitive capital markets.

I would like to comment on just one more of Mr. Hartmann's statements—the one concerning the frequency and the nature of analysts' visits after profit by industry reporting was instituted. He said: "It is interesting that their visits were not as numerous, nor as lengthy, as they had been in the past. We were providing them, in writing, with most of the information that they wanted, and their visits thus became for the most part general discussions about the future of the company."

In my experience, most analysts are more than willing to earn the opportunity to ask questions of management representatives by meticulous development of a frame of reference on the company's affairs such as will enable them to properly interpret and utilize the information they are given by management. Thus, it follows that the more meaningful material published, the less management time and effort required to bring the analyst to grips with his key touchstones of profitability, risk and growth potential. The more knowledge of the past and present available for study at home, the more of precious management visit time can be spent in dialogue on future prospects and—of key importance—the better equipped the analyst is to center his attention on the most significant areas of inquiry and to properly interpret the information he is given.

In closing I would say that this line of reasoning—the more meaningful material published the better for the investor—extends even to the Kern County-Tenneco merger proxy statement. It is a model of technical completeness and accuracy. As an investment analyst, I enjoyed poring over each of its 124 pages. It may be that few non-professional shareowners read beyond the introductory letter but I would guess that their advisers did read much further and to the great benefit of both adviser and investor.

NEWMAN T. HALVORSON

Implications of Conglomerate Reporting for the Independent CPA

I'm supposed to talk about the implications of product-line reporting for the independent CPA. Having heard the views of the SEC about the need for this kind of reporting to protect the investor, and the views of our legislative establishment about the need for it to protect competition, in addition to the views of the investment community and of management, you may wonder what there is left for me to say. I wonder a little bit about that myself.

All these points of view influence the accounting point of view. Independent accountants and corporate accountants have spent endless hours over the past year discussing and debating this reporting problem, and we have probably let ourselves get as much concerned with and involved in these legal and managerial and corporate-impact aspects of the question as we have with the strictly accounting aspects. This has become a somewhat emotional issue, and the accountant has not always been able to confine himself to what I think is his proper province.

It is difficult to avoid all this emotion and personal bias about an issue which has come into such prominence in such a short space of time, and there is a fair amount of personal bias in what I am going to say. It is also a bit difficult to isolate the accounting aspects from all the other related aspects. However, it may be less difficult to distinguish the independent-accounting aspects from the more general accounting aspects, so that's what I will try to do.

I can say at the outset that one immediate impact on the independent accountant is client reaction. Corporate managements, with negligible exceptions, are not enthusiastic about these proposals for expanded reporting, and they are not enthusiastic about having their independent auditors appearing as ardent advocates of the proposals. I sympathize with that point of view, but I have tried to not let it influence my remarks this morning.

The accounting aspects are especially dependent upon the resolution of the legal implications and the corporate problems. If the solution of the corporate problem is this, the accounting problem (or answer) is that. If the solution is that, then the accounting problem will be different. Regardless of the problem, the accountants have the competence to handle it, but we need to know the requirements first. Independent accounting is a service business, so we don't create a product and offer it for acceptance. We offer a service to meet a specified demand. And while the demand in this situation exists today in certain quarters, it is anything but a specified one.

I'm not sure that the independent accountant should be deeply involved in this movement at this time. He can be in it as a citizen concerned about social and economic progress, or as an investor concerned about learning all he can about the issuer of securities in which he has invested, but as an independent accountant, a CPA, his participation may be premature.

Once the legal implications and corporate-impact problems are settled, we should play a big role, but we shouldn't be the innovators. It has seemed to me that Chairman Cohen of the SEC, who is the strongest voice calling for this expanded reporting, may be misinterpreting the functions and prerogatives of the CPA in suggesting that we appear so much in the forefront of this crusade.

We should distinguish the role of the CPA, the independent accountant, here a good deal from the role of the internal accountant, the corporate accountant. The corporate accountant is a part of management and can and should help management make its view known on the impact of this proposal on the corporate community. Most members of the Financial Executives Institute fall into this group. It was originally The Controllers' Institute, as most of you know. We as independent accountants are enthusiastically behind that group in its present efforts to bring the issue into focus.

So to try to get these accounting aspects and impacts on the track, let's say that the independent accountant can, and probably will, play a multiple role.

He can be an instigator and innovator in promoting the extended reporting, which means to a large extent deciding what should be reported. This is the role that Chairman Cohen would apparently like us to play, but as I said before and will elaborate on later, I don't believe this is our role, or if it is, we are playing it prematurely.

A second role we can play is to decide how to report once the purpose and subject matter of the report has been agreed upon. This role we can play very effectively, always in collaboration with the corporate accountant and management, of course.

A third role we can play is to pass upon the quality of the reporting, the attest function, analogous to our present certifying of financial statements.

Another role we can play, and that we will undoubtedly be asked to play, if product-line reporting becomes a requirement, will be that of management consultant or advisor to corporations on organizational problems. Many corporations are not organized along product lines, and do not have accounting systems designed to produce product-line information. There will be a vast amount of rearranging and redesigning to be done, the amount depending on the depth to which product-line reporting will be required to penetrate. Much of this will be related to cost accounting and other directly-related accounting questions, but there will also be problems of organization structure and managerial responsibilities which the accountant is well equipped to solve in his capacity of management consultant.

To dwell again upon the first role for a moment, at the risk of being repetitious, remember that the CPA's position in respect of financial information is a secondary one; the responsibility for content, for subject matter, falls on the reporter. The independent accountant reviews it for quality.

I don't want to convey the idea that we are a static profession. We aren't, and we can innovate within our province. Financial reporting has been evolving and improving steadily and significantly, and in large part this is certainly because of the attention that the CPA has been giving to it. As a profession we recognize that we have an obligation to society to promote good financial reporting and to work for its improvement.

The SEC position in the present movement is that this expanded reporting and extended disclosure is necessary for the protection of investors, and we can agree that the interests of investors are paramount in designing general-purpose financial statements for published-report purposes. But it is the issuer of the securities who reports to the investor, and it is the issuer who is in the best position to know what the investor ought to know about the issuer's affairs. This is very much the position advocated by the Machinery and Allied Products Institute in its excellent pamphlet, *Top Management Looks at Product-line Reporting*. We must distinguish between our "report," as an attest to quality, and the corporation's report, which includes the finacial information to which we are attesting.

So the accountant's freedom to espouse is circumscribed until he learns what the demand is. We have one active exponent of special reporting for conglomerates in the person of Chairman Cohen, as has been said, but the dimensions of his requirements have yet to be defined. We have a less direct exponent, almost a "me too" voice, in the financial analysts, but their requests have been vague. Give us more! Nothing specific, just more, and we will figure out a use for it. That's not satisfactory.

The corporation can't be reporting just for the sake of reporting. It has to be for a purpose and directed towards a defined end. Otherwise the danger of misleading is as great as the possibility of informing.

When I say "defined end," it opens up a wide area for definition. We not only need to define our objective, we need to define our starting point.

Which particular reporting entities are those of whom these expanded disclosures are expected? And what should they be telling that they are not now telling? And to whom and why should they be telling it?

We need to know the need. Who wants what? The American Accounting Association, the national organization of educators in accounting, issued a booklet late last year entitled *A Set of Basic Accounting Standards*. In it the Association makes a strong point of the importance of research into what the users and readers of financial statements need. A valid proposal. That of course is an important objective of the research project presently being conducted by the Financial Executives Institute, but its project has seemed to me to be directed with greater force to determining what is available and feasible in the way of more detailed financial reporting.

In the meantime the independent accountant can only play the advisor, almost the Cassandra, to those more directly involved and responsible. He can point out the complexities and the dangers and the pitfalls, as though they were not already all too obvious to the issuer on whom the responsibility will finally rest.

Somewhere in all the comment that has appeared on this subject in recent months the rhetorical question was asked: "Who reviews a book?" The answer of course is, not the author but some unbiased critic. The intended analogy was to the role of the independent accountant in determining whether corporation reports are good or bad, with particular reference to his influence in establishing standards for conglomerate reporting. The analogy is pertinent to our role of certifying financial statements, but the critic does not tell the author what to write.

The second role I mentioned for the accountant is to decide how to report the information that conglomerates may be asked to furnish about themselves. Here I am satisfied that the independent accountant has all the competence and ingenuity required to perform once the needs are defined. The problems will range from the simple to the complex, but we can handle them.

Up to now the disclosures that have been made about product-line results and divisional operations have taken many forms, but almost without exception they have been presented as something separate and distinct from the certified financial statements. They appear most often in terms of dollar revenues only, sometimes in terms of percentages of total revenues, sometimes in terms of units of product, rarely in terms of dollar net income, and so on. They may be offered in narrative fashion or in tabular fashion, or in graphs or charts. The form has been as varied as the content. And of course the presentations have been wholly voluntary, except for certain prospectus disclosures required by the SEC.

I hope this extended reporting, if it becomes a requirement, will continue to be something separate from the financial statements proper to which the independent accountant's certificate runs. There is a body of accounting principles to which the financial statements must conform for fair presentation. They may be ill-defined in some areas, and overly flexible in others, as some of our critics maintain, but they do represent criteria against which the financial statements may be measured.

The financial statements in their entirety, including footnotes, are usually presented in as concise a fashion as is permissible within the bounds of adequate disclosure for fair presentation in conformity with generally accepted accounting principles. Anything beyond that is redundant; anything less suggests that fair presentation has not been achieved. Once an auditor has expressed his opinion that a set of financial statements presents position and results in conformity with generally accepted accounting principles, any condensation of those statements ipso facto becomes a breach of fair presentation requiring some qualification of the auditor's opinion if he is asked to report on the statements in their condensed version. Any expansion of them, if covered by the same standard opinion, suggests that the initial statements must have been something less than fair presentation. The auditor is properly wary about letting his opinion cover a variety of presentations of a given set of financial statements of any issuer without appropriate corresponding variations in the language of his opinion.

The auditor should be similarly wary about expressing his standard opinion on the financial statements of a conglomerate including disclosures of product-line information if he is going to express the same opinion on the statements of a non-conglomerate that do not offer such information. This is not to say that the presentation of the product-line information may not be in conformity with generally accepted accounting principles; it is to say that with its inclusion the financial statements present something *more* than results of operations in conformity with generally accepted accounting principles as that phrase is now commonly interpreted and understood by accountants.

Once a decision is reached about what to report and how to report, the independent accountant must decide what to do about it. This is the third role mentioned earlier. I regard it as inescapable that eventually we will be called upon to express our opinion in some fashion upon this information if it becomes required reporting. We will then need some new standards of acceptability against which to measure this specialized information to supplement the present generally accepted accounting principles against which we measure the financial statements proper.

We will also have to formulate some agreed-upon standards of performance for ourselves to supplement our present generally accepted auditing standards, which were developed with broader goals in mind than product-line and divisional results. Obviously we can't be making representations about this additional information without having audited it in some appropriate manner.

As I said, I think it is inescapable that sooner or later the independent accountant will be asked to lend his name to these extended disclosures if they become obligatory. We know that that is already true in respect of such information now appearing in published annual reports when it is later incorporated into prospectuses. In those cases the underwriters quite generally ask the auditor to bless the information in the so-called comfort letter given to the underwriters. Eventually, similar "comfort" will be expected as to the published annual report, but then the comfort will be offered to each and every user of the report.

If it should be decided that these disclosures are essential for fair presentation in conformity with generally accepted accounting principles, it is evident that we will be expressing our opinion of them in our standard report on the financial statements. This will require an exceptionally refined and precise definition of the circumstances under which such disclosures are essential to fair presentation, and would presuppose an extension of auditing procedures to cover them.

If it should be decided that the disclosures should be made in conjunction with the financial statements proper, but not as an essential part of fair presentation of financial position and operating results, we might still cover them in our report on the financial statements but distinguish them as a self-contained thing apart, as is now commonly being done for the so-called funds statement. This is a matter of technical nicety in reporting that I shan't try to elaborate on, because it is of concern mostly to the auditor himself.

If it should be decided that the disclosures shall be made outside the context of the financial statements proper, which I hope will be the case, we can take the comfort-letter approach, and offer some factual representations coupled with some negative assurance. Comfort letters now often relate to fragmented information more or less pertinent to the financial statements, so there is a pattern for this kind of reporting by the auditor.

The danger of the comfort-letter approach from the independent accounting standpoint is the lack of sophistication of the typical reader of a published annual report as compared to the sophistication of the underwriters to whom comfort letters are presently offered. Comfort letters are written in response to stipulated requirements and within mutually agreed-upon bounds. Until some corresponding stipulations are agreed upon for general application to conglomerates, reporting by the auditor may have to take some highly qualified forms.

The reporting by the corporation could be limited to strictly factual representations about what the information is, how it was derived, what the underlying assumptions are, and so on. That is the direction I would like to see it take. Very likely during the early stages of this development, that is the form it will take, because there will be no agreed-upon standards or common assumptions that will permit an *opinion* about what is presented. Fairness is not an absolute, and therefore an opinion on the quality of the information reported must await development of some standards to which it can be related.

If the reporting by the corporation is limited to such factual representations not requiring an opinion, I would hope that the independent accountant would not have to be involved. The issuer of the report would incorporate disclosure of the premises and assumptions into the presentation of the information itself, and the information would stand or fall on that basis, on its own merits. Of course, the accountant could participate in developing the presentation as he currently does in designing financial statements, including footnotes.

To repeat, whenever the independent auditor does lend his name to the reporting, it will be in his role of an attestor to the quality of what is presented. And until the standards of the presentation have been identified by reference to an objective that has not yet been defined, whatever the independent accountant says will be heavily tinged with qualifications, if not disclaimers.

What I have been saying has dealt with the reporting and auditing aspects of the problem. Reporting in the sense, first, of what should be reported and how it should or might be reported, and second, of what kind of report the independent accountant might make on the reported information. Of course, the reporting and auditing aspects are elements of the overall accounting aspects, and they are problems chiefly because the purely accounting aspects are a problem.

Now why is this all so difficult? This has been threshed out so repeatedly among accountants, both independent and corporate, within the past year that anything I say will be a cliché. Those of you who have read the excellent and comprehensive article, *Conglomerate Reporting: Friend or Foe?*, by our fellow panelist, Al Sommer, have been adequately exposed to the accounting problems. I don't know who coached Mr. Sommer on the accounting, but he surely highlighted the issues.

Dr. Solomons is going to analyze the accounting problems for us later this morning and suggest some solutions for them, and I don't want to intrude on his subject, but I hope he will forgive me for making some brief references to them now, because they are a necessary background to some of the other implications for the CPA about which I want to talk.

There are several possibilities for the presentation of income-statement information about product lines or revenue-producing activities that might be meaningful to users of the statements. For example, the disclosure might be of revenues only; it might be of "defined" profits, which in turn might be either gross margins or contribution margins; or it might be of net income after allocation of all costs and expenses, including income taxes. However, no matter what approach we take to subdividing accounting information for a diversified business, whether by product line or revenue-producing activity or geographical sector or what have you, once we go beyond the revenues there are certain problems that are sure to arise. These relate to allocation of costs and expenses for common service functions, for common productive facilities, for internal transfers of products and services, for financing costs, and for income taxes, to take the more conspicuous examples.

Revenues are no problem. Whether they are sales or service revenues, they are usually readily identifiable with some product line or with some definable activity of the business.

Costs and expenses are another matter. Many costs and expenses (maybe most of them in the typical business) are directly associated with certain product lines or certain revenue-producing activities, but in every business there are other costs and expenses (and frequently large amounts of them) that cut across product lines and revenue-producing activities and even across managerial responsibilities. They are the so-called joint costs and common costs of various kinds.

The assignment of these kinds of costs and expenses to specific revenue-producing activities requires determination of appropriate bases of allocation. Most companies make such allocations now to develop the information believed necessary by management to make its internal decisions, but there is anything but uniformity or general agreement about the bases or methods of allocation that should be followed. The allocations are arbitrary. Not in the sense of being whimsical, but each company devises its own scheme to arrive at the information that it believes will be most useful.

What are some of the implications of this for the independent CPA? I'm thinking now more about the accounting profession as a group, not the practitioner individually.

The purpose of all this extended reporting is to permit analysis and evaluation of the performance of the conglomerate company. This evaluation requires comparability, but comparability with what?

With the company's own performance in preceding years, naturally. But more important, with other businesses producing the same product lines or engaged in the same revenue-producing activities, whether they be single-product or single-activity companies, or corresponding product and activity segments of other conglomerates. But until everybody agrees on what defined profit or other objective is being sought, and on some uniform bases of cost and expense allocation, the comparisons may be illusory at best, and might often be misleading.

One of the basic charges to the Accounting Principles Board is to narrow differences in accounting, to improve comparability by making like things look alike and by eliminating alternatives. This improvement of comparability is difficult to achieve in the financial statements of businesses taken as a whole; as between businesses, that is.

It will be unbelievably more difficult if the statements are fragmented into product-line reports. The variety of circumstances that may make like things look unlike, depending on operating policies and managerial judgments, is so great that the comparability problem may be beyond solution. We are going to have more diversity instead of less.

This isn't a question of accounting principles, generally speaking. It is a question of what kind of information a business needs about itself, and the answer to that can't be separated from management's judgment and discretion. It seems quite improbable that the CPA will be able to express an opinion that these product-line reports present their information in conformity with any generally accepted set of criteria. The criteria will quite properly be self-established and self-serving, and that is not going to promote comparability between businesses.

Along with the problems of comparability between businesses, we have the problem within a business of consistency between years. When the independent CPA reports on financial statements, he is required to express his opinion on whether or not the accounting principles have been applied on a basis consistent with that of the preceding year. I have said that these product-line problems are not matters of principle, but let's assume that they are.

We can achieve internal consistency in the application of cost allocations and so on from year to year, but let's say that one of the requirements is to report separately on every product-line segment accounting for more than 15 percent of the revenues or more than 15 percent of net income. The 16 percent segment in the first year may be a 14 percent segment in the second year, and vice versa. This could keep alternating indefinitely. Would this on-again, off-again, in-again, out-again reporting be inconsistent? I don't believe so, literally speaking, if the generally accepted criterion is 15 percent, but comparability will surely be suffering.

This aggravation of the comparability problem is only one of the implications for the accounting profession. Sooner or later the APB or some similar authority (I use the word lightly) will have to decide whether we are dealing here with matters of principle and whether the disclosure of product-line information is necessary for fair presentation of operating results in conformity with generally accepted principles. As I've suggested before, I hope the answer is "no," not because I'm opposed to disclosure, but because I think there is a distinction between disclosure, which is a reporting and auditing problem, and principles, which are an accounting problem.

Another facet of this deserves attention as it relates to the single-product or single-activity company. The single-product company has a minimum of allocation problems and its conventional income statement, beginning with sales and ending with net income after income taxes, is its product-line report. The conglomerate with one segment operating in the same product line may have allocation problems of such complexity as to make a complete statement of income for any segment a practical impossibility. The conglomerate therefore decides to report on its several segments on the basis of down-to some defined profit.

Should the single-product company then be required to redesign its income statement to display a correspondingly determined defined profit to permit meaningful comparison with the conglomerate segment? In so doing it might be forced to reveal information about itself that has not heretofore been considered necessary for a single-product company. Nor is it now being proposed as necessary for the single-product company, but it might become so if the less-than-complete income statement of the conglomerate segment is to serve its purpose.

You may appropriately ask why, if so much of this desired information is being developed and presented internally in the ordinary course of business, there should be such hesitancy by the independent CPA about making it available to investors or so much protesting about the difficulties of reporting on it. One answer is, of course, that the users of the internal information know the ground rules under which it was prepared, and, besides, they are using it against a background of other information, past and current, that no investor could reasonably expect to have. The investor could not hope to get more than the briefest of summaries of the information, as compared to much underlying detail available to the management user. A little knowledge can be a dangerous thing.

Another question may be why this reporting would be so different from and more difficult than present conventional reporting to investors and other outsiders. The answer, we might say, is the converse of the allocation problem. All the intracompany transfers get eliminated when the several segments are combined for conventional reporting, and all the allocations, no matter how arbitrary and how fragmented, fuse back into their original pre-allocation unity.

Another implication of this movement to the independent accounting profession is what it does to its position regarding consolidated financial statements. As a profession we have been pushing hard, maybe too hard, for more and more complete consolidation to achieve the fairest of fair presentations. Now to adopt a principle that separate disclosure by product lines is necessary for fair presentation would certainly be a contradictory position, and probably an untenable one.

Possibly the intensive study now being given to product-line reporting will provoke a reexamination of existing recommendations for consolidation, and produce some relaxations. I believe it would be a good thing.

A corollary implication is involved in the reporting on financial statements of a component of a business enterprise, a subsidiary or a division, not necessarily a product-line activity or separable industry activity. The APB and the AICPA Committee on Auditing Procedure have been considering this question of how to report on components for several years, and haven't yet offered an answer. Certainly we will have to decide how to report on the statements of a legally distinguishable subsidiary corporation and on a practically distinguishable semiautonomous division of a business before we decide what can be done in reporting on product-line results.

My remarks have been directed pretty much to the reporting of income, or operating results, but the problems are magnified if we involve the balance sheet, and maybe we should. Product-line results standing alone, without corresponding disclosure of the related capital investment, and the composition of it, could be quite misleading. Development of this balance-sheet information by product lines may also require a multitude of allocations, many of them arbitrary.

Eventually I'm sure it will all result in more work for the independent CPA and higher fees for his client; how much is unpredictable. Obviously the client will incur substantial additional expense in developing the information, with or without the intervention of the CPA.

Frequent mention is made of the moves the United Kingdom has made to require product-line disclosures. The Companies Act as recently amended requires that where turnover is attributable to two or more what the Act describes as "substantially differing classes of business," the company must state the proportions in which the turnover is divided among the classes and the extent to which, in the opinion of the directors, each class has been profitable or unprofitable. However, as I understand it, this disclosure is not made as a part of the financial statements but in the "director's report" which accompanies the statements as submitted to the stockholders. The "substantially differing classes of business" is a very loose definition, but probably isn't too far from what we think of as a "conglomerate" in this country. I do point out that the independent chartered accountant in the United Kingdom is not yet required to certify to these disclosures.

I am sure you have seen the Statement released by the Accounting Principles Board in September entitled *Disclosure of Supplemental Financial Information by Diversified Companies.*

To give you a little background on it, let me say that the SEC first handed this problem, logically enough, to the AICPA Committee on Relations with the SEC and Stock Exchanges. That committee initially may have led the SEC and Chairman Cohen on a bit by suggesting both a willingness and an ability to comply that probably was not indicative of the then views of the AICPA as a whole, and certainly was not indicative of the views of most corporate managements.

As the complexity of the issue became more apparent, the issue was referred to the Accounting Principles Board, not so much because of the principles involved as because the APB is supposed to be the most authoritative body and voice that our profession has, and this was obviously an issue that was going to take a lot of resolving.

The APB was hesitant about taking a position on the merits of the issue then, and to a degree it still is, primarily because there hasn't been a demonstrated need for the information or any clear picture of what the information ought to be. The APB at first proposed a hands-off attitude until more research into the need for and feasibility of the program had been carried out, thinking particularly about the FEI research project which was then in the incubation stage.

That attitude changed. Partly the APB was persuaded, and partly its hand was forced (in my view), to take some action this year, and the Statement just mentioned is the result. The Statement is not one of our so-called Opinions, and in no sense is it a research study. It includes a brief recital of the kinds of presentations that some diversified corporations have made along product lines, a strong recommendation that other corporations, conglomerate and otherwise, experiment with similar presentations and disclosures in their reports, and a cautionary note about some of the accounting pitfalls that must be avoided if the information is to be valid and meaningful. It suggests the possibility of independent research of the issue by the AICPA, and also suggests that the APB may sometime issue a more definitive pronouncement.

You should understand that by virtue of this being a "Statement" and not an "Opinion" of the APB, and I put both "statement" and "opinion" in quotes, failure to observe its recommendations does not constitute a departure from recommended practice which would require disclosure in the report of a certifying accountant as would be the case if we were dealing with an APB Opinion.

For the time being, the APB is maintaining liaison with the Financial Executives Institute and is most anxious to learn the results of the FEI research, because those results may well determine the future course of the APB in this interesting area.

SIDNEY DAVIDSON

Implications of Conglomerate Reporting for the Independent CPA–Comments

In considering the role of the independent CPA in the controversy over divisional reporting, there is one crucial question that dwarfs all others. It is the question of the meaning of the central phrase in the accountant's opinion, the phrase that the statements "present fairly the financial position and results of operations." If information that is important for analyzing and understanding the results of operations is omitted, can the statements be said to "present fairly?" Does "present fairly" carry with it the connotation of full disclosure of all available, relevant information?

The judgment of how much disclosure is required for fair presentation is one that must be made by the individual public accountant or by the public accounting profession collectively. We can rely on the reassuring legalism that reporting divisional or product-line results has not in the past been held to be required for fair presentation. Or, we can recognize that financial analysis of diversified firms may be considerably enhanced by reporting divisional results. We know and are pleased that investors have placed greater confidence in financial information covered by the accountant's opinion than in unaudited data. I am sure investors would prefer to continue to rely on financial data encompassed by the accountant's opinion. But if there is financial information that investors and financial analysts feel is necessary for a full and fair understanding of a firm's performance and position and it is not included in the accountant's opinion, the investors and analysts will reluctantly but quickly become accustomed to seeking out and using unaudited data. Both the user of financial statements and the accounting profession would suffer from this change. It is a situation that the public accounting profession cannot permit to come about.

Put affirmatively, I look forward to the time when there will be full or relatively full divisional reporting by all conglomerate firms and these reports will be covered by the independent CPA's opinion. I hope we will see an Opinion by the Accounting Principles Board to this effect. These actions should come soon if the profession is to retain its position of public respect and trust.

This is, of course, my personal opinion. There are other CPA's like Newt Halvorson, whose judgment I respect, who have different feelings. We have heard Mr. Barr, Mr. MacCallan, Mr. Parker, and others describe the need for divisional reporting. What reasons lead some CPA's to oppose divisional reporting, or at least the inclusion of divisional reports in the data to be covered by the accountant's opinion?

The loudest complaints are usually reserved for the problem of allocating joint costs among the several divisions. It is clear, of course, that this problem does not arise on the income statement unless we go all the way to determining net income. It is nonexistent or negligible in measuring "defined profit." But if we seek full reporting all the way to net income, the question must be confronted. In many cases, probably the great majority of them, the amounts involved are not likely to be material. There will be some cases where the amounts are significant, however, and in those instances it would be wrong to minimize the conceptual problem involved. Allocation of this period's costs that are joint or common to several divisions to specific individual divisions is an enormously difficult, virtually intractable problem. In fact, it is almost as difficult and intractable as the problem of allocation of depreciation to specific individual years. I suggest that the cost of all durable equipment is joint to the several accounting periods that benefit from the use of the equipment, and there is no conceptually satisfactory, generally accepted way to allocate it to individual periods. All joint cost allocations are arbitrary; none can be said to follow logically the economic facts. Yet we've been calculating depreciation in a more or less acceptable fashion for a long time. Our present income statement contains a goodly number of joint cost allocations. Will one more matter?

I am reminded of the most apt comment of George O. May that the reporting of business income for short-time periods would be indefensible if it were not indispensable. The same may well be said of divisional income reporting.

There is one big difference between the two joint cost situations. In the divisional reporting case, differences in allocation procedures will affect the amount of net income for the several divisions, but not the amount of corporate-wide net income for the year. Differences in depreciation allocation procedures, on the other hand, affect the amount of reported net income, year by year.

I would hope that we will not be in too much of a hurry to specify "generally accepted accounting principles" with regard to the allocation of joint divisional costs. To paraphrase Professor Solomons' suggestion, CPA's should accept any consistently applied, systematic and rational plan of allocation, so long as a company makes clear what it has done. After all, we have been allocating the joint period cost of plant in a variety of systematic and rational ways for some time now. We have not even required a statement of which of the multitudinous permitted depreciation methods was used by the reporting firm; I hope Accounting Principles Board Opinion No. 11 or 12, now being exposed, will be enacted in December and remedy that reporting deficiency in depreciation. I trust that we will not slip into that error again, and any official stand on allocating joint divisional costs will call for full disclosure of methods used.

I share Professor Solomons' optimism that there will be a reverse Gresham's Law effect and with the wisdom of experience, good methods of allocation will tend to drive out bad, and reasonable quantities of uniformity will emerge.

The more basic question to me is not whether we can devise reasonably effective means of allocating joint divisional costs, but whether we should. Professor Solomons has wisely pointed out that the main goal of divisional reporting is "the enhancement of the predictive value of accounting information which is likely to result when the past and current performance of each segment of a business is known rather than just the overall results." Those of us who are skeptical of the information enhancement that results from the overhead allocations of absorption costing and thus favor direct costing, are similarly skeptical in this case. However, as long as we report both defined profit (contribution margin) and net income by divisions, we can satisfy the informational needs of both groups of analysts. The results are likely to be as uniform and objective as those we obtain in many other reporting areas today.

The notion of adding another element where we lack uniformity is disturbing to many CPA's, recalling the basic charge to the APB to narrow the areas of difference in accounting practice. But note that divisional reporting will not increase the difference in the reporting of corporate-wide income. In the important area of divisional results, we do *have* uniformity at present—the uniformity of being uninformed.

Perhaps I confess my primary academic background by saying that I find Mr. Halvorson's comment that "a little knowledge can be a dangerous thing" a completely unsatisfactory guide to policy in this area (and probably almost every other area as well). If the question is important and is being considered by investors, I would say some knowledge is better than none and considerable knowledge is even more desirable. In place of our present uniformity of a complete lack of audited information about divisional operations, I would prefer some knowledge on how the firm itself views these results of divisional activities. Of course, I would prefer to have these reports presented in a way that permitted easy comparison among firms. However, as long as the organization, goals, and operating methods of multi-divisional firms differ, such easy comparability will be a long-time development—a development that can be hastened by having each firm report its divisional operations in the way that seems best under its circumstances. Comparisons of methods will facilitate narrowing the range of alternatives. If we put off taking any action until we can get uniform results, it is likely that we may never get any action. I am not sure that would displease some of those who emphasize comparability.

There remains the question of whether this is a problem on which the Accounting Principles Board, the official professional spokesman for independent CPA's on questions of accounting principles, should take a stand. Mr. Halvorson and many other CPA's say "there is a distinction between disclosure, which is a reporting and auditing problem, and principles, which are an accounting problem." This is not a new type of question here or abroad. The question of whether sales had to be reported as the opening figure on the income statement or if we should start with an intermediate profit figure was settled some time ago in the United States after some heated discussion that was not too unlike our current consideration of divisional reporting. During the year I spent in England in the mid-50's, one of the hottest questions for debate among accountants was the compulsory reporting of turnover (sales).

Mr. Halvorson probably goes farther than most when he says that "it is the issuer of securities who reports to the investor, and it is the issuer who is in the best position to know what the investor ought to know about the issuer's affairs." I could not disagree more. The investor is in the best position to say what he wants to know about the issuer's affairs and it is the certified public accountant, upon whom third parties rely, who must decide how much disclosure is necessary to "present fairly." Sufficient disclosure for fair presentation is a basic accounting principle—one upon which the public accounting profession must insist, one upon which the Accounting Principles Board should speak.

The Accounting Principles Board did take a meaningful step in this direction in the Statement released in September. Mr. Halvorson says that "partly the APB was persuaded to take some action this year and partly its hand was forced." He and I probably differ on the relative strength of the parts. As one of the members of the Board who was trying to persuade and who obviously has little power for hand forcing, I am inclined to attribute almost all of it to persuasion and a recognition by the Board of its social responsibility. The Board accepted the idea put forth so well by Mr. Halvorson when he said we are not "a static profession. . . . As a profession we recognize that we have an obligation to society to promote good financial reporting and to work for its improvement." "Financial reporting has been evolving and improving steadily and significantly." I would add that the next step in that steady and significant evolution and improvement is to have divisional reports included in the financial statements covered by the accountant's opinion.

DAVID SOLOMONS

Accounting Problems
and Some
Proposed Solutions

We have left far behind us the classical concept of "the firm" as an entrepreneurial unit controlled by its profit-maximizing owner or owners, operating in a geographically restricted area, and supplying a single product in response to a given demand. The modern corporation bears little resemblance to this simple picture. It operates on a world-wide scale; it markets thousands of products; and it does not accept demand as given but creates and controls it, within limits, through marketing expenditures.

Its diversification is one of the most striking respects in which the large modern corporation differs from the classical model of the firm, and the trend in this direction shows no sign of slowing down. Indeed, to the extent that it is reflected in the number of mergers and acquisitions which are reported, it seems to be gathering momentum. There were 2,377 mergers reported in 1966, while 1,416 were reported in the first half of 1967, with a predicted total for the year of 2,600.[1] Many of these mergers undoubtedly have diversification as their main motive, both as regards products handled and geographical areas served.

While it is easy to distinguish conceptually between diversification of the evolutionary type, where new products or businesses are added as natural developments of the old, and diversification through the acquisition of unrelated businesses, it is not so easy in practice to say whether a particular addition falls into one category or the other. The expansion of the Columbia Broadcasting System and its affiliates is a case in point. The line from CBS radio to Columbia records, and hence to the Columbia Record Club seems natural enough, and so does the line between television and films. Broadcasting and musical instruments are not wholly unrelated, so the acquisition in recent years of companies making violin strings, guitars, and drums can be explained. The Columbia Record Club's mailing list

[1] *Wall Street Journal*, July 6, 1967.

91

might reasonably explain the group's recent move into the mail-order business through the acquisition of Sunset House. But can the acquisition of Holt Rinehart be regarded as a natural development on the ground that broadcasting and publishing are both concerned with communication? And is the acquisition by CBS of the New York Yankees natural because they are both in the entertainment business? It is just as easy to answer Yes as No to these questions.

DEFINITION OF CONGLOMERATE UNNECESSARY

Though it seems commonly to be thought that the true conglomerate, resulting from a series of acquisitions, presents a more acute and urgent problem of financial reporting than does the other case, which might be called "volutionary diversification," in fact it is much easier to legislate for it. It is clear that the less closely related the various activities of a corporation are, the easier it is to account for each of them separately. The difficult problems are those relating to the allocation of common costs and of shared assets and the treatment of inter-divisional transactions. Obviously the more disparate the activities of the divisions are, the fewer costs and assets they will share, and the fewer transactions they will have with each other. Fortunately, therefore, the investor's most acute need—the unscrambling of the results of the substantially unrelated activities of the true conglomerate—is also the easiest to meet, as the Chairman of the SEC recognized in his statement, in September 1966, to the Senate Subcommittee on Anti-Trust and Monopoly.

Unlike some of those who gave evidence before the Senate Subcommittee,[2] or who have discussed the matter since, I see no reason to attempt to define a conglomerate, or to distinguish in any clear-cut way between the two types of diversification. It surely cannot be contemplated that any new disclosure requirements would be imposed on the conglomerates but not on other diversified companies. The investors' needs are much the same, however diversification comes about; and in any case, after a few years, acquired subsidiaries are just as much "part of the family" as new ventures which are developed internally. Any new disclosure requirements, it seems to me, must be drafted in general terms, so as to apply to all companies; but different companies would be differently affected by them, according to their degree of diversification and, as I shall suggest, their internal structure.

OBJECTIVITY VS. RELEVANCE

Other participants in this symposium will have weighed the benefits and costs of reporting financial results by company segments. In considering the methods by which such reporting may most effectively be done, it is important to keep before us the main purpose to be attained, namely, the enhancement of the predictive value of accounting information which is likely to result when the past and current performance of each segment of a business is known rather than just the overall results. If some of the

---

[2] For a discussion of this evidence, see A. A. Sommer, Jr., "Conglomerate Disclosure: Friend or Foe?," *supra*, pp. 1–16.

resulting figures (e.g., some expense allocations) are not completely objective, this is no reason for denying the usefulness of the results. The trade-off between objectivity and relevance in accounting is going on all the time, and there is nothing unusual in the discovery that to increase the relevance of reported company results there has to be some sacrifice of objectivity.

Some writers in this field seem to be concerned, too, at the absence of "generally accepted accounting principles" relating to segmental reporting.[3] But if this were to be considered fatal, accounting would have to stagnate, for if new developments had to await general acceptance before they could be introduced, most of them would be still-born. Let us get on and resolve the problems of segmental reporting, for out of the ferment, the general acceptance of some solutions as being better than others may be expected to result.

A QUESTION OF EQUITY There is a question of equity between companies which calls for early recognition, for it has a bearing on the solution of the problems under discussion. Mr. Manuel Cohen drew attention to one aspect of it, in the statement to which I have already referred, when he pointed out that a percentage test as to what constituted a segment the results of which must be separately stated might allow a large division of a very large company to escape disclosure because it was a small part of the whole, while a much smaller division of a smaller company might be required to disclose its results because percentage-wise it formed an important part of its company's business. Issues of equity also arise in connection with the information which it is decided shall be disclosed. For instance, if companies were required to leave central administration and research expenses unallocated, as a pool of expense to be covered out of divisional contributions to overhead and profit, companies which had delegated most functions to divisions would show relatively small divisional contributions as compared with those who had delegated fewer functions and who had large corporate administrative and research staffs. The divisional "profits" of these latter companies would look relatively high. This result is not always palatable to the companies concerned, as the pharmaceutical industry, with its heavy basic research expenditure, will testify.

The fact is, of course, that a grave inequity is perpetrated by *not* requiring the reporting of segmental results, for companies making a narrow line of products may feel at a disadvantage compared with more diversified companies. A good example is Maytag, specializing in home laundry

[3] Cf. Professor Robert K. Mautz, in his article, "Conglomerate Reporting and Data Reliability," *Financial Executive*, 35, No. 9, September 1967, p. 31. "There are at present no generally accepted principles of accounting related to the allocation of common costs among segments of a company . . . if management, in allocating common costs, has used assumptions entirely appropriate to its purposes, on what basis does the independent accountant find them faulty? . . . until 'generally accepted principles' of allocations for external reporting are established, how does he show the impropriety of what may be quite rational assumptions?"

equipment. Its principal competitors are no more than subdivisions of the major appliance division of companies like General Electric, Westinghouse, and the Frigidaire Division of General Motors. Maytag's results are of considerable interest to the home laundry subdivisions of these companies, wheras Maytag can learn little from its competitor's accounts.

It is doubtful, of course, whether any product-line reporting which is likely to be required of its competitors in the foreseeable future would benefit Maytag, because even if G.E., Westinghouse, and the others disclose figures for major appliances, home laundry equipment will probably be merged with dishwashers, refrigerators, ranges, and other appliances. Except for a prospective entry into the dishwasher market, Maytag does not handle these other appliances.

Behind these questions of equity between company and company lie the two fundamental questions which call for answer:

1. What is the reporting unit to be, for which diversified companies must separately disclose results? What is the relevant segment that we should like to isolate?
2. What information is to be disclosed?

Neither of these questions admits of easy answer, and most of the discussion hitherto has been more concerned with asking questions and pointing out difficulties rather than with offering solutions. It is more fun to ask questions than to give answers. But perhaps by now we have enough questions and should turn to look for the answers.

SEGMENTS OF VARIOUS KINDS Bearing in mind that the purpose of requiring the reporting of company results by segments is to put investors in a position to make better informed investment decisions, it can be argued that any aspect of a business, separate information about which would materially influence an investor, ought to be the subject of separate reporting. There is no logical reason for being satisfied with divisions or product lines as the sole basis for segmental reporting. *Where* a company does business is of great concern to its stockholders and potential stockholders, also, especially when an important part of its business is done abroad. Reporting earnings by geographical source is an accounting service which investors should welcome.

Geographical segments of a business are as difficult to isolate as any other kind of segment. The problems of shared expenses and assets and of intersegmental transactions are always with us. But though entirely satisfactory solutions to these problems have not yet been found and perhaps finally cannot be, an increasing number of companies are already distinguishing in their financial statements between the results of domestic business and overseas business. As recently reported by Professors Berg, Mueller, and Walker, of the University of Washington,[4] in an admittedly

---

[4] "Annual Reports Go International," *Journal of Acountancy*, August 1967, pp. 59–64.

small and statistically non-random sample of large U. S. companies having a substantial amount of foreign business, only two out of twenty companies gave no financial information about their international business. Fifteen of the twenty gave either dollar figures for net sales abroad or the percentage of total net sales made in international markets; and twelve gave either dollar figures for foreign net earnings or the percentage of total net earnings derived from international markets. The authors report considerable lack of uniformity in defining these terms and in arriving at the reported results, the differences of practice relating principally to the treatment of export sales from the U. S. and the way in which the activities of non-consolidated international subsidiaries were handled. However, the important point is that the investor's interest in the geographical source of his present and prospective dividends is recognized by most of these companies, and his need for something more detailed than total consolidated earnings is on the way to being met. A more detailed geographical breakdown than that between the U. S. (or in some cases North America) and the rest of the world is only the next step, and one already taken by some companies.

There is one troublesome aspect of this type of segmental reporting which differentiates it from product-line reporting and which was much discussed in Britain during the recent debates over the new Companies Act there, in connection with the Act's requirement that companies shall report the value of goods exported.[5] In Britain the main motive seems to have been to give publicity to companies which were making a full contribution to the improvement of the balance of payments situation. More rationally, one could argue that investors should know how their company's fortunes are likely to be affected by developments in various parts of the world. The difficulty is that a company may be exporting *indirectly*, without knowing it, by selling material to another company at home which then exports it in the form of a manufactured product or otherwise.

The British solution was to require direct export sales to be reported, leaving companies free to give additional information about indirect exports, if they were able to and so wished, in the directors' report to stockholders or the Chairman's speech. This seems a sensible procedure. Thus a hotel chain, with no direct exports, might well report how many visitors from foreign countries it had accommodated, and what it thought its earnings from them had been. The stockholders could hardly fail to be better informed as a result.

Yet another type of segmental reporting which investors might find useful would be between business transacted by a company with private customers and business transacted with public authorities at local, state, and federal levels. One obvious reason for wanting such information would be to assess a company's dependence on defense activity, and to estimate

---

[5] Companies Act 1967, sec. 20.

the impact which an outbreak of peace might have on it. Unfortunately again, as with export sales, sales to public authorities might be made at one or more removes, as a sub-contractor rather than as a prime contractor, and perhaps without the company even knowing to what use and to whose use its products were being put. It would be easy enough to require companies to report separately sales which they know to be destined directly or indirectly for public use, and earnings thereon. For the reason already mentioned, complete objectivity and precision, even in reporting sales, would not always be possible; but even if only direct sales to the public sector were reported, the investor would surely be better informed than if such figures were not disclosed.

To anyone who thinks that divisions or product groups are the only kind of sub-entity worth bothering about for reporting purposes, this discussion will look like a digression. However, the point should be emphasized that there are many dimensions to the question of reporting sub-entity results, and information which may be useful to the stockholders of one company may not be useful to those of another. However, it is probably safe to say that if satisfactory ways to report divisional results can be found, some of these other problems will be solved as by-products. For instance, work on defense contracts by large companies tends to be concentrated in a small number of divisions, and though some government work may be found in all divisions, the bulk of it will be found in a few. Thus the disclosure of divisional results will also show where the impact of government activity falls most heavily.

HOW IS THE REPORTING UNIT TO BE DEFINED? The first question about divisional reporting to be settled is how the reporting unit is to be defined. Should the financial statements presented to the SEC and to stockholders be allowed to follow a company's own organizational structure, reporting as a division (or, in the case of some very large companies, a group of divisions) whatever the company calls a division or group? The Chairman of the SEC does not (or, at least, did not) think so for he said, in his statement to the Senate Subcommittee, "Clearly the unit indicated on a corporate organization chart will not always be acceptable." The only alternative I have seen suggested is that companies should be required to report their results in accordance with some more or less broad standard classification such as the Standard Industry Code of the Census Bureau. The main argument for this proposal is, of course, that it would facilitate inter-company comparisons, segment by segment.

I do not like this suggestion. I think that a company should be free to choose whatever divisional or departmental structure it thinks most suitable to its circumstances, and having chosen it, it is natural that the accounting statements prepared for the guidance of management should follow and reflect this structure. If these statements, as we must presume, are the best that management can produce to guide their own decisions, then there is an initial presumption that the same statements, or less detailed versions of them, are likely best to serve the investor in making his investment and disinvestment decisions. Whether the same can be said about labor unions and government agencies, in the use they make of a company's financial statements, is perhaps doubtful. But our focus, in this discussion, had better be on the interests of the stockholders, at least initially.

The use of the Standard Industrial Code or anything like it as a basis of financial reporting to stockholders is unattractive for several reasons. It would represent a major departure from any existing practice for, as Mr. Cohen points out, the Code is applied for statistical purposes by the Census Bureau to individual plants, not to companies, and in any case it is used only as a classification of output, not earnings. It bears little or no relation to the way that most companies keep their own accounting records, so that to adopt it as a basis for external reporting would mean that companies would have to choose between a non-preferred basis of cost and revenue classification and keeping duplicate records, one for SEC purposes and one for their own. Neither alternative is desirable. Moreover, unless by accident the standard classification corresponds to a company's own divisional organization, or unless the SEC is to be content with the reporting of gross margins on product lines, leaving all overhead unallocated, then a reporting system which departs so radically from the company's own internal structure must call for a proliferation of arbitrary expense allocations. In the result, therefore, there might be a gain in inter-company comparability; but the results being compared would have lost significance in the process.

The inclusion of "always" in Mr. Cohen's statement makes it impossible to disagree with it *in toto;* but I should hope that there would be few instances where the company's own organization could not be accepted as the basis for financial reporting. However, this view carries with it the corollary that the company has an obligation to explain its organization and to describe the activities of its divisions. The better annual reports to stockholders already do this. Companies could also be required to certify that the classifications used in their financial statements correspond with the principal centers of profit responsibility recognized in the company's internal structure, and this certificate could be corroborated by the auditors, who would naturally have become familiar with the company's structure in the course of their duties.

Whatever definition of product line or division is chosen, there will be problems. The question has been asked whether General Motors would be expected to report sales and earnings separately for their five passenger car lines because these cars are marketed by separate divisions, or whether the relevant category would be passenger cars as a whole.[6] If the Standard Industrial Code were used as the basis of accounting, no distinction would be drawn between one General Motors brand and another. This is one

---

[6] Sommer, *loc. cit.,* p. 11.

example where following the company's organization chart relentlessly would lead to more detailed financial reporting than would the use of a standard statistical classification, and perhaps more detailed reporting than stockholders would find useful. Of course the number of vehicles sold by each division of the major automobile manufacturers is already made known publicly each quarter, in any case. The General Motors case perhaps suggests the need for a company to be able to apply to the SEC for some relaxation of the rule I have put forward, that the classifications used in the company's financial statements should correspond with the principal centers of profit responsibility which it recognizes, where this would call for an unreasonable degree of disclosure. It would be most regrettable if any accounting regulations, because of their inflexibility, were to lead a company to change its internal organization and control procedures simply in order to avoid a degree of disclosure it thought unwarranted.

Another related question which Mr. Cohen asks is "how important a particular division must be in the overall picture of a company before separate earnings figures should be required." His reasons for regarding a percentage test alone as unsatisfactory have already been mentioned. The answer seems to be to use a two-prong test based on net sales. Any division which had net sales of more than $X or whose net sales to outside customers represented more than Y% of the company total would be required to be separately reported, with the net earnings therefrom. Companies would of course be left free to use lower limits, with consequently more detailed reporting. Presumably the SEC is only concerned with *minimum* standards of disclosure. But this would still leave a loophole for companies which would like to avoid reporting divisional results, for we have not yet defined the distinguishing characteristic of a division. If sufficient heterogeneity in a division's activities is allowed, the whole concept of a divisional structure becomes eroded; and if a very high degree of homogeneity is demanded (so as, for instance to split an electric lamp division into two, one making incandescent lamps and the other the fluorescent variety), then by means of a finer and finer breakdown, all "divisions" could become small enough to swim through the net of reporting requirements. It would be a mistake to try to legislate for this too closely. Few companies surely would seriously distort their managerial structures merely to evade some reporting regulations; and assuming this to be so, it seems enough to rely on the directors' certificate, already suggested, to the effect that the financial statements (with attached notes and schedules, of course) reflect the principal centers of profit responsibility recognized by the company's management structure. But to backstop this arrangement, let the SEC have powers to question the correspondence between the financial reports and the management structure, and as a last resort, if it is not satisfied, let it have the power to require that the company present its financial report in accordance with some approved standard classification. This sanction should be enough to keep companies in line.

ACCOUNTING PROCEDURES FOR SEGMENTAL REPORTING

The SEC has always shown a commendable reluctance to impose particular accounting methods on companies or to veto methods it did not like if it could avoid doing so. It is to be hoped that it will continue to take this approach to the problem of determining divisional sales and especially divisional profits. The emphasis should be on seeing that companies disclose the accounting procedures they have used in arriving at the results reported, rather than on dictating what those procedures should be.

In accordance with this approach, which would permit wide latitude in the choice of accounting method at the price of full disclosure of what has been done, it is unnecessary to prescribe, for example, whether and in what way central research or administrative expenditures are to be allocated to divisions, so long as a company makes clear how it has handled these expenses. Most discussion of the difficulties of segmental reporting has centered on this question of the allocation of corporate expenses, without much regard to their quantitative importance. In fact, they do not often represent more than 5 percent of a company's total expenditures; but even so, they may constitute a substantial proportion of a division's net income, and certainly enough to change the picture of a division's profitability.

Many different ways of handling these non-divisional expenses can be devised. A uniform basis for allocating them in total, to be used by all companies, could be laid down by the SEC; or a different uniform basis for each category of expense could be imposed on all companies; or uniform bases for each category of expense could be laid down, industry by industry, with a different set of bases for each industry—if anyone can devise a way of assigning a conglomerate to an industry; or any allocation in external reports could be prohibited, leaving divisional net earnings to be shown as contributions to corporate expenses and net profits; or companies could be left free to choose their own way of presenting the facts of the situation, as they see them, on condition, of course, that they explain clearly what they have done. I have already expressed my own preference for the last of these courses. I am also optimistic enough to think that, before long, good methods of handling this problem will drive out bad, and a large measure of uniformity will be secured without the need for regulations.

Besides the treatment of corporate expenses, there is quite a list of items, in fact, which will need to be the subject of explanatory notes. A few of these items will be mentioned shortly. But even taking a latitudinarian approach such as is advocated here, there is a need to prescribe one or two rules in the interest of uniformity. We can leave a broad area for individual freedom and yet stop well short of anarchy.

INTER-DIVISIONAL TRANSFERS

One such rule would relate to inter-divisional sales. There are at least three possibilities as to how divisional sales might be reported. One is to report total sales by divisions, combining sales to outside customers and to other divisions. A second is to report inter-divisional sales and outside sales separately. The third is to eliminate inter-divisional sales, reporting only sales to outsiders. It is equally easy to adopt any one of these alternatives, but the best procedure seems to be to eliminate inter-divisional sales from reports to stockholders. This is really equivalent to saying that all materials or products transferred between divisions shall be transferred at cost, including a proportionate share of overhead. The result will be to leave each division to bear the cost of goods sold to outside customers, and it would report sales to outsiders and the costs thereof.

As a consequence of this procedure, important divisions which work mainly or perhaps wholly for other divisions of the company—the Fisher Body Division of General Motors might be an example—would disappear from the financial report, except to the extent that they had sales to outside customers. All earnings would be attributed to the divisions which market the final products. The result would be the same as if all stages of making the final product were carried on in the end-product division. For the purposes of financial reporting to stockholders, this is not at all an unsatisfactory result, whatever may be thought about it from a managerial point of view. It brings together in one place the profit which the company has extracted from a particular market—the market for Chevrolets, for instance, or all passenger cars, depending on how closely the financial statements follow the organization chart—without regard to the way the company has chosen to organize the manufacturing facilities used to serve this market.

If at first sight this appears to be inconsistent with the view put forward earlier, that the reporting regulations should conflict as little as possible with the accounting needs of the company's own management structure, a closer look will show that transfers only exist because products are made by one division and marketed by another. Only if all transfers could be valued at market prices established in perfectly competitive markets would it be possible to set up an external reporting system which gave the stockholder objective figures of divisional earnings which were consistent with the way that the company organized both its production and its marketing activities. But since such a basis for transfer prices is not always available, a choice has to be made. Pricing transfers at cost has the effect of attributing all profits to marketing activities, so the reporting system is made to conform closely to at least that side of the company's profile.

Where transfers of services take place between divisions, these should also be accounted for at cost. This is already an almost universal practice, and enforcing this as a rule for external reporting purposes should not give rise to any problems.

Pricing transfers at cost (including divisional overhead) means, of course, pricing them at average cost. To the extent that a division's cost of goods sold includes transfers from other divisions, therefore, it cannot be said that the division's profit—or even its gross margin—represents the diminution in corporate profit which the company would suffer if the division were closed down, nor will its results, by simple extrapolation, indicate the effect on corporate profitability of an expansion or contraction of the division's operations. The reason for this is that, since the cost of transfers charged to the transferee division includes costs which are fixed from the point of view of the transferer division and therefore from the corporation's point of view as well, the company's total costs will not increase proportionately with an increase in the volume of transfers taken by the transferee division.

This conclusion may be disappointing to those who think that it is easy to provide investors with measures of divisional contributions to corporate profitability. It is not easy, for this and for other reasons which will be referred to later. But there is no cause to be unduly discouraged merely because divisional results are subject to the same limitations as are the corporate results. No one expects corporate net profits to bear a constant relationship to sales, and therefore to be capable of prediction from a simple extrapolation of sales. At the most, the use of average cost for pricing transfers to a division simply extends to the measure of divisional results the limitations which already apply to the corporate results.

It is worth adding that, in the majority of diversified companies, interdivisional transfers are small in amount when compared with sales to outside customers, and it is easy to exaggerate the difficulty which they put in the way of measuring divisional performance. There are many companies in which the whole question could be forgotten without any serious distortion of the accounting results; and the broader the company segment which is chosen as the reporting unit, the more likely is this to be so.

TAXES ON DIVISIONAL EARNINGS
Another matter about which it seems more appropriate to prescribe a procedure rather than simply to require disclosure as to a company's own choice of procedure is the treatment of taxes on divisional earnings. Stockholders are interested in having an approximation of the contribution which each division makes to the company's fortunes, so that it is divisional after-tax earnings which should be shown. It is not enough to divide up the corporate tax bill between divisions in proportion to their before-tax earnings, unless the same relationship between accounting profits and taxable profits exists for all divisions. If it does, there is no need to allocate taxes to divisions. If it does not—if, for example, some divisions attract depletion allowances and others do not—then taxes should be charged to divisions as nearly as possible in accordance with the amounts they would bear if they were separate businesses; and if a division shows a net loss, the tax relief which the company will enjoy as a result should be credited to it.

It has been pointed out to me that most divisions which attract depletion allowances are likely to be divisions making intermediate products for transfer to other divisions. This is probably true. If inter-divisional sales are eliminated from the financial statements, as was suggested above, then the income-tax charges or allowances relating to these intermediate divisions will have to be charged or credited to the divisions which market their products, in proportion to the value of transfers taken by each end-product division. This treatment seems to be consistent with the rationale of the treatment of inter-divisional transactions already proposed, in that it brings together in one place all of the profit extracted from a particular market, regardless of the manner in which the company chooses to divide up the responsibility for its production and marketing activities.

OTHER MATTERS TO BE DISCLOSED

Perhaps there are other matters relating to divisional accounting for which procedures should be prescribed by the SEC; but it is to be hoped that the list of rules could be kept to a minimum. The price to be paid for this relative freedom from regulation is maximum disclosure as to the bases used in arriving at divisional sales and earnings. The need for an explanatory note about the treatment of central administrative and research expenditures has already been mentioned. Other matters which need to be explained to stockholders if the significance of divisional earnings is to be understood include the following:

1. Any charges which have been made by corporate headquarters to divisions for services, interest on capital, occupancy of premises or the like, and how any such charges have been computed.

2. If the recommendation made above that inter-divisional transfers should be accounted for at cost is not adopted, it will be necessary to explain how they have been valued and charged for. Generally, where transfers are not made at actual cost, the basis used will be either at market price, where one exists, or at market price less the selling expenses saved on internal sales, or at standard cost or some variant thereof. Occasionally incremental cost is used, but this is rare. The explanatory note on transfer prices may have to be somewhat lengthy, unless uniform procedures are used throughout the company, not an entirely common situation. This reinforces, perhaps, the case for eliminating transfers from the financial reports by accounting for them at cost.

3. The treatment of all non-operating gains and losses, such as gains and losses on the disposal of fixed assets, fairly attributable to particular divisions should be explained, especially if they have not been credited or charged thereto.

It will be said that to leave so many accounting matters to be decided by a company's management will greatly increase accounting disuniformity and impair comparability between companies, and to some this seems to outweigh everything else.[7] This I believe to be a short-sighted view. The most important quality in an accounting statement is the degree of correspondence between the picture it presents and the facts of the situation it

---

[7] This seems to be the view, for instance, of Mr. Keith Goodrich, as expressed in his article, "Executive's View of Corporate Reporting Responsibilities," in *The Financial Executive*, **34**, No. 12, December 1966, esp. p. 20.

represents. Comparability with other statements is a secondary, not a primary quality, and it will no doubt develop as we gain experience of segmental reporting. So long as each company discloses its methods and follows them consistently, investors cannot fail to be better informed, even if uniformity between companies suffers in the short run. In any case, the serious consequences of disuniformity flow from the failure of companies to disclose their accounting methods rather than from the differences among the methods themselves.

REPORTING DIVISIONAL INVESTMENT

The demand for divisional or product-line reporting does not stop at the reporting of sales and earnings. Investment or capital employed in each division must also be shown if stockholders are to be informed about the rate of return on investment from each division. Here again, companies have a good many choices open to them as to how divisional investment is to be computed, and the important thing is that the particular set of choices which have been made should be explained. Most fixed assets can be allocated directly to divisions, leaving usually only the corporate office building and the central research facilities, which are best left unallocated. Inventories and receivables are usually capable of direct allocation also. The company's cash balance is a function of many considerations, some of them unrelated to divisional behavior. It can well be left unallocated, as should any outside investments held by the company.

In computing the investment base for *corporate* Return on Investment calculations, a choice has to be made between using stockholders' investment or total investment. Whatever choice is made for corporate purposes, in comparing *divisional* rates of return it seems best to use total divisional assets as the investment base. In any case, the treatment accorded these matters in the company's financial statements needs to be explained.

There is one respect in which it is easier to compute the investment base for external reporting purposes than it is when the purpose is management appraisal. When top management uses Return on Investment as a measure of the performance of divisional management, the distinction between the expenses and assets which are controllable at divisional level and those which are not is important, and it is not always an easy distinction to draw. For the purposes of external reporting, however, it is the performance of a division's business, not of its management, which is of primary interest, and controllability at levels of management below the top is not a relevant consideration.

THE IMPACT OF DIVISIONS ON EACH OTHER

It is the impact of divisions on each other which gives rise to some of the subtlest problems of performance measurement in a divisionalized business, problems which in the present state of the art are more often sidestepped than solved. For instance, a division produces a material both for its own use (or for sale to outside customers) and for another division. The quantity taken by the transferee division enables the producing division to spread its overhead and reduce its average unit cost. If transfers are made at cost, there will be no routine accounting measure, in the accounts of either division, of the benefit to the producing division from the economies of scale resulting from the production it transfers to the other division.

Inter-divisional benefits flow, too, when one side of a company's business brings revenue to one of its other activities. We have seen this exemplified recently in the scramble by the airlines to acquire or build hotels in countries which they serve. The ownership of Intercontinental Hotels by PanAm and of a large number of Hilton Hotels by TWA are the best known examples of this kind of integration. There is no doubt that some of the income generated for the group by the airline will show up in the accounts of the hotels, and some of the income generated by the hotels will take the form of increased sales of airline tickets. Some of these benefits of integration will no doubt remain with the division that generates them through commissions charged by one division to another on business brought in. But it is also certain that there will be more indirect benefits which will not be traced to their source.

Many other examples of this kind of integrated diversification could be cited. The Hilton Hotel Corporation is said to be considering going into the automobile rental business. Bell & Howell, already important in the field of visual aids for education, is going into educational publishing. The New York Central Railroad has recently expanded its hotel interests. There will be inter-divisional benefits from these developments for which no precise accounting is likely to be possible in the foreseeable future.

CONCLUSION I draw attention to this matter to deflate any exaggerated hopes that divisional or product-line reporting will give stockholders accurate information about the contribution which each segment of a company's business is making to its fortunes; and the same point has already been made in connection with the pricing of inter-divisional transfers. To recognize this limitation is not to surrender the case for reporting segmental results. If we were to be satisfied with nothing less than perfect accuracy in the field of profit measurement, we should have to abandon the task altogether. But with all its shortcomings, no one can doubt that the investing public, though sometimes misled by accounting failures, is on balance immeasurably better off with the financial reports which it gets than it would be without them. And so it will be when segmental or divisional reporting becomes the rule rather than, as now, the exception.

MICHAEL N. CHETKOVICH

Accounting Problems

and Some

Proposed Solutions–Comments

Professor Solomons has presented a thoughtfully considered paper, one which speaks from the depth of study he has devoted to this subject. Nonetheless, it illustrates the complexity and uncertainty surrounding the subject at the moment. Although he does take on a number of the problem areas, one still is left with the impression that there are more questions than answers, and that where solutions are posed they require assumptions or qualifications. This is by no means a criticism of his paper, but rather is indicative of the present state of the whole issue of reporting by segments.

It is a temptation, in this particular discussion, to restrict oneself to an analysis of some of the more significant accounting problems raised by Professor Solomons. One could speak at length on the pros and cons, the methodology and problems relating to such issues as transfer pricing and cost allocations. However, even a preliminary consideration of the accounting problems brings with it a recognition that, before reasonable judgments can be made as to the most appropriate accounting methods to be applied, there must first be a much clearer delineation of the objectives.

While the subject of segmental reporting has received a great deal of attention of late, there seems to be very little consensus yet as what is to be accomplished and for whom. Professor Solomons recognizes the need to define objectives, for he says that, in considering methods, "it is important to keep before us the main purpose to be attained" which he concludes to be the "enhancement of the predictive value of accounting information." He goes on to pose what he considers to be the two fundamental questions which call for an answer:

"What is the reporting unit to be. . .?" and

"What information is to be disclosed?"

He again gives recognition to the importance of defining the objective by stating that the focus, for his discussion at least, "had better be on the interests of the stockholder."

Even if we could agree that the goal we are striving for is the enhancement of the predictive value of the accounting information to the investor, we still would be left with significant areas for further consideration, such as what kind of information and how much will be useful to the investor, and to what degree, and the related questions of availability and reliability of the information and the possibility of adverse consequences.

Professor Solomons makes certain other assumptions or conclusions as prefaces to suggested solutions for the questions raised, such as that there is no great need to define a conglomerate or to distinguish between cases of diversification arising from acquisitions on the one hand and from internal development on the other.

This conclusion again demonstrates an awareness of the need to keep in mind the objective to be attained. Definitions and distinctions of this nature are significant only if they are relevant to the attainment of the objective, or if the terms are to be used in connection with determination of rules or regulations which may be proposed to be applied.

Professor Solomons poses the need for recognition of the question of equity between companies in determining the type and degree of information to be disclosed. This may pose an interesting conflict of purpose, for is it not possible that the main purpose claimed, that is aid to the investor, may not be served if relatively insignificant data is required (which may obscure the more essential data), solely because of considerations involving equity between companies? Reporting for the investor should be considered in the light of his requirements. Equity as between companies merits consideration in the determination of requirements which may be imposed by governmental or other agencies, but it should not be permitted to obscure consideration of the best means of attaining the principal objective.

The question of the segment to be reported on is a basic one and Professor Solomons quite rightly devotes considerable attention to it. He points out that there is no logical reason for accepting divisions or product lines as the sole base for segmental reporting, if the purpose of such reporting is to put the investor in a position to make better informed investment decisions. Again, this underscores the importance of considering the purpose in determining the nature of the information to be reported.

Professor Solomons goes on to discuss the possible significance of reporting earnings by geographical source. This discussion illustrates the difficulty of generalizing on any aspect of this subject. While disclosure of results of foreign operations is generally of interest to the investor it is questionable whether there is comparable pertinence with respect to geographic areas within a country. Does East versus West or North versus South have any real relevance to the investor? Even the extent and manner of reporting foreign operations requires consideration in terms of relevance to the investor. What is it that is pertinent to the investor here—is it the volume or profitability of foreign operations overall or is it more specific areas of concern, such as degree of risk? There may be a wide divergence between areas of foreign operations in terms of risk, currency restrictions, market potential, etc.

There is another problem of geographic reporting that deserves attention. Production within one country and sales in another pose a different kind of risk and accounting problem than production and sales within the country. For many companies these situations are not discrete, and therefore are difficult to separate.

This is not to say that there should not be disclosure of foreign operations, but, rather, that the method and degree of such reporting requires consideration in the light of the particular circumstances.

Another illustration of the difficulty of generalizing on the type of segmental reporting has to do with the reporting of business transacted with governmental units as against that transacted with private customers. Professor Solomons points out that one obvious reason for such reporting would be to assess the company's dependence on defense activity with its attendant uncertainties. However, we all recognize that a mere reporting of transactions with governmental units versus private customers would not necessarily accomplish this or any other worthwhile objective. For example what would be accomplished by a company in the school supplies business breaking down its sales according to public schools versus private schools?

Again, each situation must be considered on its own merits—and in terms of the objectives to be attained. As Professor Solomons says very pertinently, "the point should be emphasized that there are many dimensions to the question of reporting sub-entity results, and information which may be useful to the stockholders of one company may not be useful to those of another."

As to how the reporting unit is to be defined, there is merit to Professor Solomons' suggestion that this be correlated with the company's organizational structure—so long as reporting along this line has relevance in relation to the objective to be attained. Certainly, this would seem to be preferable, if we must generalize, to reporting in accordance with some arbitrary classification such as the Standard Industrial Code. However, again, each situation must be considered on its own merits. The presumption that information most useful to management is likely best to serve the investor requires careful study. It can be argued very cogently that the management objective of best allocating and managing the resources of a company requires information considerably different in character from that required by an investor for best allocating and managing his investment resources.

Companies may, of course, be segmented structurally even though they may not be diversified in so far as product lines are concerned. Thus a company may be structured along functional lines—production, marketing, research, administration, etc. Or, it may be structured along geographic lines. In many of these instances, any attempt to report financial information, particularly profitability, externally along organizational lines would be a meaningless exercise. Little, if anything, would be gained from attempting to segment the external financial reporting of a fully integrated operation.

Let us now consider some of the more specific accounting problems which are faced by Professor Solomons and his suggested solutions. His preface to this discussion, to the effect that emphasis should be on disclosure of methods or procedures in arriving at amounts reported, rather than on dictating what procedures should be, is realistic, as is illustrated by his consideration of the handling of non-divisional expenses. While there might be (and I say might advisedly) a presumption that if a choice of a single method of allocating such expenses had to be made, one could be selected which would have the widest applicability, there still could be a great variety of situations in which it would not be applicable—or certainly would not represent the best method in the circumstances.

Little would be gained from the imposition of an arbitrary rule for and method of allocating non-divisional expenses as compared with the misleading implications and difficulties which could result. And, while the amount of such expenses might not be material in relation to the whole in most instances, as suggested by Professor Solomons, still there are situations where such expenses may be significant, particularly in relation to the profitability of certain units.

INTER-DIVISIONAL TRANSFERS Professor Solomons suggests that this is one area where rules might be prescribed in the interest of uniformity, and that the best procedure would seem to be the elimination of inter-divisional sales from reports to stockholders. He points out that this is equivalent to saying that transfers should be made at cost. It is not too difficult to subscribe to this conclusion if one assumes this *is* an area where uniformity is necessary, and so long as the user of the information recognizes that this method does not necessarily provide the best measure of divisional profitability.

As Professor Solomons so aptly points out, it is not easy to provide investors with measures of divisional contributions to corporate profitability. It is quite likely that, in certain instances, misleading inferences as to relative profitability would be drawn as the result of pricing inter-divisional sales at cost. A given division might be made to look more or less "profitable" than it in fact would be if it were operating as a separate entity. For example, a division which produces a product which is both sold to an outside market and used as a raw material by another division might well be able to sell its entire output commercially. If this is so, this division's "profitability" is affected adversely by transferring its product at cost, while the transferee division benefits from this procedure. Management is in a position to recognize this possible inequity and may, for its purposes, use some other method of transfer pricing to better measure the relative performances of the two divisions. However, the investor probably will not be able to make a similar distinction.

Implicit in all of these considerations is the need to recognize that the reporting of results by segments has to be considered in the context of the whole organization; it does not necessarily provide a fair measure of what the segments might accomplish as separate entities.

TAXES ON DIVISIONAL EARNINGS   This is another area where Professor Solomons considers it more appropriate to prescribe a procedure and recommends that divisional after-tax earnings be shown, at least in those instances where there is considerable variation in the relationship between accounting profits and taxable profits.

It is quite likely, as Professor Solomons suggests, that the stockholders would be most interested in after-tax earnings. However, it must be recognized that here, as in many other areas of segmental reporting, there can be considerable difficulty in making meaningful allocations, particularly where the product which attracts the unusual tax treatment (such as percentage depletion) may both be an end-product and a raw material transferred to other divisions. The situation can be further complicated by such factors as investment credits, deferred taxes, operating losses, etc. Again, if income taxes are allocated, the result may not necessarily be indicative of what the particular division would have incurred, by way of tax expense, if it had been a separate entity.

OTHER MATTERS   There are, of course, other areas of accounting for divisional operations which merit consideration. One of these, which often proves troublesome in practice, is interest—both expense and income. Should only interest expense actually paid be allocated—or should interest be imputed to all segments and, if so, what disposition should be made of the credit? The allocation of research and development expenses can be particularly difficult. There are many other areas which could be mentioned, but time does not permit.

Professor Solomons states that "the demand for divisional or product-line reporting does not stop at the reporting of sales and earnings," that "investment or capital employed in each division must also be shown if stockholders are to be informed about the rate of return on investment for each division." This, too, is an area which requires careful study before any conclusions are reached as to what should be reported and how. There is considerable debate over the relative validity of the various means of computing the rate of return for the total entity, let alone its segments. Intelligent use of rate return statistics requires a knowledge of the underlying circumstances, and under certain conditions the publication of such information, even with explanatory disclosure, could be more misleading than informative.

SUMMARY   In reflecting on what I have said here, the general impression may well be that the presentation has been negative—that more problems are raised than solutions posed, that it is more critical than constructive. If so, it is, as I have said before, in no way a reflection on Professor Solomons' excellent paper, but rather, as far as I am concerned, is a reflection of the present state of this whole question of segmental reporting.

I feel a considerable sense of frustration in trying to pose constructive conclusions as to what should be done, and I believe that this feeling is shared by many who have addressed themselves to this subject. Perhaps it is pertinent, at this point, to cite an excerpt from the statement of Chairman Cohen of the Securities and Exchange Commission to the Senate Subcommittee on Anti-Trust and Monopoly in September 1966:

"While the problems facing us are not insurmountable, they are difficult problems, and I do not believe we will find simple answers to them. Their difficulty suggests that we must proceed with deliberation and with a recognition that experience may prove to be our best guide in reaching the most appropriate solution." [1]

The question of segmental reporting with all its attendant problems is receiving a great deal of attention and study by various agencies, organizations, and individuals, and by corporate management. Even if we agree that the objective of amplification of the reporting on diversified operations is a meritorious one, the questions of how much and how require much study. Progress is being made, and it would seem that the orderly approach to a reasonable resolution of this problem involves continued study, coupled with experience in practice, along two lines:

1. A consideration in depth of the needs of the investor for additional financial information, in terms of what kind of information and how much, by the various interested agencies, industry and professional organizations, and others.
2. Consideration by managements of diversified corporations, on a company by company basis, of how they might best amplify their reporting to their shareowners, giving consideration to all the circumstances involved in their particular situations.

Professor Solomons has stated that "the most important quality in an accounting statement is the degree of correspondence between the picture it presents and the facts of the situation it represents." Thus, the most productive approach to the problem, certainly for the present, would appear to be a case by case analysis by those in the best position to understand the particular circumstances of each case, that is the management of the company, leading to a reporting which is responsive to their best judgment of

---

[1] Statement of Manuel F. Cohen to the Subcommittee on Anti-Trust and Monopoly, Committee on the Judiciary, United States Senate, September 20, 1966.

the situation, coupled with a much more thorough delineation of the overall objective to be attained.

We have seen a considerable increase in the incidence and degree of segmental reporting in recent years and it seems reasonable to assume that the near future will see a significant acceleration in this trend. It would be a step backward, in my opinion, to impose rigid and extensive requirements for segmental reporting at this time. As Chairman Cohen stated, "experience may prove to be our best guide."

A significant contribution to the consideration of this subject has and will continue to be made by experts from the academic community. Professor Solomons certainly is one of the leaders in this group. His research and writings have shed much light on this subject and it is hoped he will continue to give it the same kind of attention.

Synthesis of Discussion

DEVELOPING A FRAMEWORK FOR DISCUSSION

When this symposium was conceived in the Fall of 1966, the focus of the demand for improved financial reporting by conglomerate corporations seemed to be on the "product line." Subsequent statements made by those concerned with this issue—underscored by near-consensus in the discussion sessions at the symposium—suggest that "product line" is too restrictive a term. It does not seem to provide a basis for meaningful discussion of ways to expand the content of financial reports of conglomerate corporations.

Product-line reporting is *one* of the methods which conglomerate corporations might use to expand financial report content. But geographical markets, industry classifications, divisions, successive stages of manufacturing and distribution, and many other ways of partitioning corporate activities also could be considered.

Consensus of the participants in the symposium suggests that meaningful discussion of methods to amplify public reporting policies of conglomerate corporations can take place only within a broader framework such as "segmental" reporting rather than in narrower terms such as "product line."

There are those, however, who argue that even "segmental" is not an appropriate framework for discussion. Fruitful discussion, they would argue, must explore more fundamental questions like the types of disclosures needed for specific kinds of decisions. Segmental reporting, some argue, may expand financial reporting by conglomerate corporations without enriching the information content in such reports.

DEFINING INTERESTED PARTIES

Those interested in improving public reporting by conglomerate corporations represent diverse interests and positions, including management, stockholders, investors (and other representatives of the investment community such as professional financial analysts), government, independent certified public accountants, and academicians. These groups are directly

113

and indirectly interested in the problem at hand, and the interests of each group overlap those of others. Representatives of government, for example, may be interested in the extent to which financial reporting practices of conglomerate corporations enable them to serve the public interest through antitrust analysis or public disclosure requirements. But this direct involvement of representatives of government may be reflected also as indirect interests of all responsible citizens who are included in the other categories of interested parties.

Managers in conglomerate corporations may be expected to be intimately concerned with the problem of devising financial reporting techniques which will facilitate self-appraisal or -evaluation. Managers also will be interested in devising reporting techniques which will enhance their ability to allocate the conglomerate organization's resources among its various components. Such interests will be tempered with concern that public reporting of the financial operations of their organizations might give comfort to competitors. Usually, however, management introspection and caution does not preclude generalized concern for public policy.

Independent certified public accountants, of course, may be presumed to be concerned most intimately and directly with the "fairness" of representations implicit in published financial statements, with respect to third-party publics interested in the results of their client corporations' activities. Thus, certified public accountants have a direct interest in and concern for public policy as well as a concern for improving their clients' abilities to evaluate performance and to allocate resources within the organization.

Investors, of course, are interested primarily in maximizing returns on investment over some suitable time horizon. Some investors will seek only their own counsel, while others will seek the advice of professional financial analysts. Professional financial analysts, of course, are interested in encouraging management to use financial reporting techniques and procedures which most effectively facilitate analysis of investment opportunities. Investors and their financial analysts are interested in projections of expected rates of return against probable degrees of risk and uncertainty. In the broader sense of a free investment market, investors and financial analysts are implicitly interested in facilitating optimal resource allocation in the economy as a whole. In general, all the parties at interest are concerned with encouraging further research in the matter of internal as well as public reporting of the activities not only of conglomerate corporations but of corporations in general.

Although the diverse needs of these groups of individuals was acknowledged, the focus of much of the discussion was on the needs of the investor and to a lesser extent on the needs of public policy decision makers for information to facilitate such activities as antitrust analysis. Most participants seemed to agree that government has the general power to request and obtain data it requires for various purposes, and therefore discussions of the informational needs of the investor may be assessed without reference to the needs of public policy decision makers.

Statements were made by participants expressing the antitrust position that segmental reporting of the operations of conglomerate corporations would facilitate the implementation of public policy by enhancing the antitrust analysis, particularly in connection with the Clayton Act. It was contended, for example, that such data would be helpful and is needed to prevent the concentration of economic power, and that regularly available reporting of activities of conglomerate corporations on a segmental basis would serve to improve judgment as to whether a government cause of action was indicated. Several times it was stressed that segmental data would not be the only data required, but that it would be very useful when used in conjunction with other information. In spite of this emphasis, several participants expressed doubt that segmental data would be useful for antitrust analysis. But those participants most directly concerned with matters of public policy emphasized that segmental reporting is crucial to day-to-day enforcement of antitrust policy.

ASSESSING INFORMATION REQUIREMENTS

Although the question of segmental reporting of the operations of conglomerate corporations dominated the discussions, there was a persistent concern with the broader and more fundamental question, "What information do users need?" Some of the participants suggested that information needed by users must be a function of the various decisions they must make, and that different standards or tests of the adequacy of information will exist for these various decisions. Investors and their financial analysts, for example, need to evaluate the prospective profitability of an investment. But even though some analysts and investors believe that segmental reporting of the activities of conglomerate corporations would enhance their ability to make such evaluations, not all participants in the seminar subscribed to the view that such information would be useful for such purposes.

The participants acknowledged that there are many varieties of informational needs, but that insufficient fundamental research has been done to determine the optimal informational needs for various types of decisions. We do not know, for example, what sets of information will best facilitate the comparison of corporate performance or the comparison of divisional performance within a corporation. We do not recognize *best* methods for evaluating management performance or for measuring the profitability of resource employment. Some participants suggested, for example, that financial reporting alone does not suffice for internal management performance evaluation, and that it should not be considered sufficient for investor appraisal of the effectiveness of a particular corporate investment.

THE ROLE OF ACCOUNTING INFORMATION

In the discussion of various informational needs, the participants examined the role served by accounting information and by the certified public accountant. Some emphasized the historical nature of accounting information, and the group was urged not to overlook the importance of the stewardship function of accounting. It was acknowledged that historical accounting information in many cases may also serve adequately as a guide to future behavior. In this sense, accounting information may be predictive in nature. It was acknowledged, however, that in some cases accounting data generated to serve a predictive purpose should be different from accounting data derived to discharge the stewardship function. In this connection, it was pointed out that although accounting data are relevant for many decisions, they should be supplemented by other information which would enhance decision making ability. In response to a suggestion that the deterministic framework of accounting limits its usefulness as a predictive mechanism, the comment was offered that even a deterministic presentation of probabilistic data would be better than no presentation at all.

IMPLICATIONS OF EXTENDED DISCLOSURE

The question of whether imperfect and incomplete information is better or worse than none at all has, of course, broader dimensions. And this question—with its broader dimensions—concerned many of the participants and pervaded much of the discussion. Many of the participants expressed a fear that public disclosure of segmental information about conglomerate corporate activities could be extremely harmful not only to the corporations themselves but to the entire economy. Fears were expressed that "professional troublemakers" among the investment group (typified by those stockholders who delight in harassing management at stockholders' meetings) would find a cause for destructive criticism and would hinder management efforts if too-detailed information on corporate activities were published. Others suggested that more complete financial disclosure would tell only part of the story, and that it would be technically impossible to tell "the whole story" in the context of published corporate financial and annual reports. Pursuit of this line of thought implies that the information required to make intelligent management and investment decisions is so extensive that it cannot be made available generally to a wide group of investors, and that only management (and, perhaps, sophisticated financial analysts who are privileged to discuss corporate affairs with management) will be capable of making intelligent investment decisions.

Another variant of these positions is that were it possible to publicly reveal "complete" information, its quantity would be of such magnitude that it could only confuse. Only the very sophisticated financial analyst could digest and interpret such proliferation of data, and proposed segmental reporting techniques would lead to an "intellectual elite" who would then possess an unfair advantage over other investors and would be in fact "insiders."

An extension of the arguments against broadened public financial reporting by conglomerate corporations suggests that incompetent analyses by investors or their representatives would inevitably lead to a misallocation of resources in the economy because investment decisions would be made on the basis of improper interpretation and evaluation of expanded information.

Fears that expanded information disclosure would lead to misallocation of resources by either confusing the would-be investor with excessive detail or misleading him by not providing "the total picture" were countered by other participants who argued that increased secrecy in managerial decision making constituted not only an impediment to the rational allocation of resources in the economy but a dangerous threat to the free-enterprise system. As one participant suggested, free exchange of information, with the attendant and implied responsibility for investment decision resting in the individual investor, is the foundation on which the free-enterprise capitalistic society rests. In principle, any policy which impairs the ability of the investor to have access to financial information is contrary to public policy.

A fundamental philosophical question is implicit in both positions. Intelligent reporting of financial operations of conglomerate corporations is highly technical, and great sophistication is required for perceptive analysis. But the principles of free enterprise suggest that responsibility for analysis and interpretation rests with the investor, and if he is unable to work intelligently with freely disclosed financial information, the responsibility for the unwise investment which would result rests solely with him. It is precisely for this reason that much of the attention of the participants was focused on the needs of the investor group, because some participants felt that as a group the investor class is not in a position to protect itself. Therefore, in the opinion of some participants, the interest of the investor should be protected by appropriate legislation insuring him free access to detailed financial information. Furthermore, a few participants argue that decisions as to which information might be relevant should be legislatively or administratively determined by governmental organizations.

Consensus of the participants seems to indicate that, regardless of the disposition of the issue of segmental reporting, there is an inevitability of "more." Most participants agreed that there are pressures demanding more complete disclosure of corporate financial information, and some participants recognized the accounting profession's unique responsibility to assist in finding a solution which will satisfy these demands. The issue seems to be: Can corporate management and its accountants present information which is superior to that now possessed by investors and which will give them a better basis for decision making? On the particular issue of segmental reporting, one participant suggested that the short-run risk that segmental reporting might lead to misunderstanding of certain companies would be justified by the incremental information which would be made available for well-conceived investment decisions.

UNIFORMITY VS. FLEXIBILITY   Awareness of the inevitability of "more," coupled with directed attention towards problems of segmental reporting (as one device by which "more" might be achieved), led the group to consider whether financial reporting standards should be uniform or flexible, and whether they should be voluntary or prescribed. In discussing these issues, one overriding question appeared: Can one set of standards—one set of information requirements—serve a multiplicity of uses and users? Context was provided by one discussant who pointed out that when he considered the problem of serving antitrust policy and investor needs, it appeared to him that an attempt was being made to serve two problems with one solution—a procedure which could only lead (and had led) to confusion. After pointing out that there can be no common solution to the diverse informational needs of investors and antitrust analysts, another participant observed that the confusion on this point originated when Senator Hart called upon Chairman Cohen of the Securities and Exchange Commission for advice on a problem which was essentially antitrust in nature. The Securities and Exchange Commission, it has been pointed out, is interested in investor protection.

Some participants expressed views during the discussions which appeared to suggest that if expanded disclosure of financial information is adequate for the investor's purposes, it will generally be satisfactory for antitrust analysis. Underlying this thought was the basic hope, if not the presumption, that a uniform reporting format would be consistently followed by the diversified or conglomerate company and that this format would have the force of regulatory compulsion behind it.

Both the participants who advocated uniform standards for segmental financial reporting and those who espoused the cause of flexibility agreed that many challenging problems must be solved before expanded segmental reporting can be implemented. Questions like the proper definition of a segment for financial reporting purposes and the extent to which costs should be allocated to segments are fundamental and must be resolved. Those who espouse the cause of uniformity argue that intersegment comparison and meaningful interpretation of financial reports cannot be made unless uniform standards are prescribed which define segments for which reporting shall be accomplished and which specify the extent and the basis on which costs shall be allocated to segments. Comparability, it is argued, cannot exist without uniform reporting standards.

The opposing viewpoints, which were subscribed to by a majority of the participants, are that individual managements are in the best position to portray their organizations to investors, and that fundamental questions like the definition of a segment and the extent and basis for cost allocation should properly be decided only by management. Advocates of the "flexible" approach to expanded segmental corporate reporting acknowledge that flexibility will undoubtedly accommodate a diversity of procedures, but they argue that this diversity is necessary to reflect the essential differences that exist among companies. As one security analyst commented, segment comparability is not easily achieved by any specific or unique set of procedures. Enforcing uniform procedures may indeed mislead users by causing them to believe that comparability has in fact been achieved. This, he argued, is a greater danger than would result if each company were allowed to decide upon its own format and reporting procedures. One participant suggested that the best way to present an organization to the investing public would be to depict the organization as perceived by its management. The degree of difficulty of implementing this approach will vary, of course, depending upon whether conglomerate organizations have grown internally or by acquisition.

Those who argued for uniform reporting standards tended also to be sympathetic to the position that such standards should be prescribed. Only by prescription, they argued, could standards be enforced and meaningful segmental reporting achieved. Voluntary reporting, they alleged, would not significantly improve the standards of public financial reporting for conglomerates. This view was challenged by some who believed that if stockholders merely were to demand segmental reporting it would be furnished.

Those advocating uniform reporting standards also tended to believe that such already existing classifications as the three-digit Standard Industrial Classification would provide a sufficiently broad and yet not too narrow base for enabling intersegmental comparisons of operations of different corporate entities. Others argued that such classifications, because they were not designed for this specific purpose, would foster non-comparability and would result in poor investment decisions because they would be misleading.

The participants examined the possibility of compromise, but the consensus (not unanimous) at the end of the discussion periods seemed to favor flexibility over uniformity. There was no clear consensus on the issue of whether voluntary or prescribed standards should be devised, but there did appear to be a consensus (again not unanimous) that a single set of standard classifications would not be sufficient to serve both the needs of the investing community and the needs of antitrust legislation.

Some consideration was given to the question of whether segmental information should be available as a regular part of published annual reports, or as a separate supplement available upon specific request.

THE BRITISH EXPERIENCE Germane to this discussion is the position taken in Great Britain toward a parallel problem. There, management is required to divulge information about the performance of various segments of conglomerate-like companies, but the decision as to whether the company is "conglomerate-like" or not, as well as the decision of the nature and extent of information to be disclosed, is left to the discretion of management. A statement covering the British experience is presented in Appendix B at the end of this discussion summary.

THE ROLE OF THE SECURITY ANALYST Related to the problem of defining and enforcing standards of financial reporting for conglomerates is the status of the emerging profession of the financial analyst, with its concomitant discipline problems. In the course of the discussions, it was acknowledged that the financial analysts are an "emerging" profession, and that—as in other professions—internal discipline must be achieved to add assurance that wise analysis of financial statements is made. At the present time, it might be suggested that the precise role of the security analyst vis-à-vis corporate management still is somewhat unclear. The search for improved standards of financial reporting necessarily demands a definition of the role of the security analyst. Formulating rules for financial reporting requires profound understanding of the corporate organization as a concept and of individual organizations in the economy. Such formulations must assume clearly defined roles for the financial analyst, and must relate his activities to those of management.

This point was vividly illustrated in the discussions. Those with reservations about new segmental reporting, particularly participants representing the management standpoint, cited not so much the potential consequences of antitrust or other actions initiated by governmental bodies as the consequences of incompetent analyses by some security analysts. Several exchanges between executives and security analysts attest to the importance of this point in influencing management attitudes toward expanded disclosure. It was emphasized that security analysts must ultimately implement standards governing their work just as CPA's do. Security analysts generally agreed on this latter point and claim to be actively working to promote general standards. The recently initiated Chartered Financial Analyst examination was cited as evidence of progress in a profession that is still in its embryonic stages of development.

SEGMENTATION AND ALLOCATION PROBLEMS

The problem of defining uniform reporting standards—or even suggesting flexible ones—is complicated by the fact that there are so many approaches to segmental reporting. From the outset of the discussions, there was near unanimous (if not unanimous) agreement that reporting by product line was neither the only possible way to partition an organization for reporting purposes, nor in most cases would it be an appropriate way.

There are, of course, many ways of focusing on the parts of an organization. It may be analyzed by its authority structure, but few seemed to believe that this would provide a satisfactory basis of segmentation for financial reporting purposes. On the other hand, some participants offered the view that in the case of some organizations and in some contexts, responsibility lines might provide a suitable basis for segmental reporting procedures. Such lines would be particularly appropriate for companies which had achieved such effective decentralization of authority and responsibility of major corporate efforts that sub-corporate entities were virtually autonomous.

The possibility of using Standard Industrial Classifications has already been mentioned. Most participants agreed that in some cases—for some organizations—this would constitute a satisfactory approach if the classifications were sufficiently broad. But in other cases, it was argued, this classification structure would not be rich enough and would inevitably encourage attempts to compare segments which were in fact not comparable.

Other methods of segmentation exist. Segmentation by geographical structure, by legal entity, or by type of distribution were named as several of the various possible bases for segmentation. Again, however, it was acknowledged that no one of these methods would be generally suitable for all cases. The extent of diversity in existing practices reinforces this position. A survey by one of the participants reveals that some corporations publicly report separately such amounts as sales in the United States, sales of foreign origin, sales by division, market, or product, and in a very few cases, operating profit by division, market, or product. Specific examples of existing practices in segmental reporting are provided in Appendix A. It is interesting to note that although some conglomerate corporations provide in their annual reports a variety of detailed segmental data, such data is usually provided in the context of the "President's letter" or supplementary material, and not in the formal financial statements.

Even if the question of defining a suitable general basis for segmentation could be resolved, it was the contention of many participants that there are other equally vexatious problems which need to be resolved. Among the most important of these is the depth to which allocations of revenue and expenses might be necessary. When considering such problems as evaluating comparable returns on investment, it might even be desirable to attempt to allocate assets among various segments of an organization—a truly heroic endeavor.

Allocations, at best, are frequently arbitrary. One participant emphasized the potential dangers of allocating with a succinct statement supplemented by examples, as follows:

"It is important that the investment analysts understand that there are certain important areas of some conglomerates which are really not susceptible of measurement in terms of operating divisions. Any attempt to do so can be and should be challenged. I am familiar with a number of conglomerates who, as a matter of fact, manage their businesses in such a way that substantial joint costs of financing, research and development, general administration, income taxes, and similar items are managed completely independently of the divisional operations. The business itself is based on the operating philosophy that the operating divisions should contribute certain profits. The overall management is concerned with providing them with capital, top-grade staff and new products.

"Under these circumstances, any attempt to allocate or attribute these expenses to divisions is purely arbitrary. Furthermore, we all know there is *no* advantage in reporting *large* divisional profits, because domestic and foreign competition, labor and the Government would all become inquisitive. Since management can attribute these expenses to any division they want, their decision is not capable of cross-check unless some criteria or standards are developed. They could certainly challenge any methods we developed. Here are a few examples to illustrate the seriousness of the allocation problem."

Contribution to Profits Before Joint Expenses and Taxes	Division A	Division B	Division C
	$5,000,000	$1,000,000	Break Even

The Company needs $20,000,000 in Division C. If it sells debentures at 7 percent, should C be charged interest of $1,400,000? Suppose A had used $20,000,000 internally-generated funds—are these interest-free to A, or should A and C be charged interest on an overall basis?

What if they decide to sell $20,000,000 of common stock to finance C? Then there is no interest expense. Are C's profits better by $1,400,000 for this reason? Perhaps $20,000,000 could be obtained for overseas operations at 8 percent and let C have other funds. What should C be charged? All? Some? None?

Research and Development of $2,000,000 for Products of Division D

This illustrates the point that research and development in this Company are undertaken for new products. They have nothing to do with the operations of A, B or C. In fact, research is performed because the products of A and B are becoming obsolete. It would be completely up to management to decide which division would handle the new products. Why should any of the other divisions be charged for research and development on the new product? What if research and development are charged to divisions on the basis of sales, and all divisions go on strike but A. Would A then be charged with all research and development costs? You could do it any way you wished.

Conversion of $20,000,000 5% Convertible Preferred of B Because of New Stock to be Issued for Company in D

This illustrates the point that, if financing costs were part of divisional operations, $1,000,000 a year would have been charged to Division B because convertible preferred was issued for its acquisition. Would its profits go up $1,000,000 if this stock were called in in connection with an overall new issue of stock to acquire D?

"The purpose here is to illustrate that conglomerates' operations can be divided—but only to the extent they are managed and accounted for on a decentralized basis. Any attempt to be precise beyond this point is questionable. How can we say that $————— per common share is attributable to divisional operations when profits are really earned on an incremental basis? We need some new math first!"

It is worth noting that some participants made the point that at this time we have no authoritative empirical studies which give us a clue as to how significant the common cost phenomenon is. Several participants believed that whenever common costs were significant (in relation to sales, but more importantly in relation to net income), segmental reporting might be more misleading than informative. Underlying this belief, of course, must be the assumption that segmental results will not be presented on a "defined profit" or contribution margin basis, but instead on a basis where some significant proportion of common costs would be allocated to segments.

MANAGEMENT PERFORMANCE MEASUREMENT

Central to the issue of expanded public reporting for conglomerate operations is the fact that no unique set of standards exists by which investors can appraise management performance. Participants in the seminar who were sympathetic to management points of view wondered whether fuller disclosure of financial and operating information to the public might not result in a shareholder "referendum" at the end of each year which would operate to the long-run detriment of the corporate organization if management's long-run plans did not meet the short-run needs of some investors.

While some participants viewed the concept of a stockholder "referendum" as an impediment to rational resource allocation and investment decision making, others sympathetic to "democratic" management viewed this as a desirable consequence of segmental reporting. Proponents of this view protested that management must not keep the investor uninformed about his investment. If certain corporate segments are expected to lose money in the short run in the interest of serving long-run stockholder welfare, this information should be revealed by management so that the stockholder might himself decide the merits of the case.

Subsequent discussion suggested that investors need not be interested in individual corporate projects, but that when projects of monumental significance were at issue (for example, General Electric's venture into the computer field and RCA's color television efforts), meaningful disclosure should be made available. It was pointed out that in such cases investment counselors and financial analysts have as important a responsibility for rational resource allocation as does management. In this context, several security analysts indicated that segmental reporting was necessary for the assessment of the reasonableness of management's earnings projections.

SOME ADDITIONAL IMPLICATIONS OF SEGMENTAL REPORTING

Related to the issue of fuller disclosure of information necessary to facilitate such activities as "stockholder referenda" is the problem of protecting the corporate enterprise and stockholder investment from competitive activity. Many management participants felt that more comprehensive disclosure of financial information might give comfort to competitors, both domestic and foreign. Management's concern over this problem and its reluctance to divulge extremely detailed information about company operation sometimes cause security analysts to complain that management is often too vague and evasive in its interviews with them. Some participants dismissed as illusory management's concern about revealing information to competitors, pointing out that corporate espionage is a fairly well-developed art.

Some of the financial analyst participants voiced the opinion that some corporations give preferential treatment to some analysts and investors, and they suggested that such discrimination could be eliminated if segmental information were routinely provided in published corporate financial reports.

Another dimension of the problem of achieving expanded disclosure of financial information relates to the behavioral implications or aspects of such disclosure. Segmental reporting of revenue and expense items, if fashioned along internal management or divisional authority lines, can have direct impact on the behavior of individuals in the corporate structure. In many cases, it is alleged that serious harm might be done to internal corporate activities if financial operations were reported along segmental lines differing from the internal corporate structure or if different transfer pricing policies were followed for external reporting than are followed for internal purposes. Yet, existing internal structures might not suit the needs of investors.

In connection with this point, some management participants questioned the wisdom of reporting on a segmental basis at a time when their own internal segmental analyses need improvement. Constantly changing internal information systems were offered as evidence of this concern. (In passing, it is worth noting that in the minds of some participants segmental reporting is seen as a vehicle for maintaining decentralization of decision structures in the corporate organization.)

One of the management participants admonished the group at the symposium that measurements cost money. Mindful of the inevitability of "more," the point was made that it would be technologically possible to furnish any kind of information that might be desired by the investing public or by any other of the corporation's publics. But such information would not come without cost, and might—in the context of cost-benefit analysis—be detrimental to the stockholder. While recognizing that expanded financial reporting for conglomerate corporations may be inevitable, it would be desirable if such expansion were to follow as closely as possible the needs of corporate management for internal information systems. By implication, uniform and prescribed standards of reporting would not fulfill this criterion.

Until formats for additional disclosure are agreed upon, the cost of processing additional information cannot be definitively determined. Management representatives did point out, however, that many if not most diversified organizations have developed responsibility accounting systems, and that reporting requirements with other than responsibility center classification could be implemented only at further cost.

Examples of

Segmental Reporting

CONTINENTAL OIL COMPANY
ANNUAL REPORT 1966

1966

GROSS PROPERTY ACCOUNTS
MILLIONS OF DOLLARS

Eastern Hemisphere, Canada, and Other Western Hemisphere

United States

'57 '58 '59 '60 '61 '62 '63 '64 '65 '66

CAPITAL EXPENDITURES
MILLIONS OF DOLLARS

Eastern Hemisphere, Canada, and Other Western Hemisphere

United States

'57 '58 '59 '60 '61 '62 '63 '64 '65 '66

EXPENDITURES FOR PETROLEUM PRODUCTION
MILLIONS OF DOLLARS

Eastern Hemisphere, Canada, and Other Western Hemisphere

United States

'57 '58 '59 '60 '61 '62 '63 '64 '65 '66

		1966
Revenues	Sales—Refined petroleum products (excluding excise taxes)	$ 772.9
	—Excise taxes collected	145.4
	—Crude oil	463.6
	—Natural gas	58.1
	—Coal and related activities	83.5
	—Plant foods	140.0
	—Chemicals and plastics	166.1
	Other sales and operating revenues	69.9
	Nonoperating revenues	15.1
	TOTAL REVENUES	1,914.6
	Purchases of crude oil	443.5
	Funds derived from operations	256.4
Income and Dividends	Net income	115.6[2]
	Dividends on Preferred Stock ($2.00 per share) [6]	4.1
	Net income applicable to Common Stock—total	111.5[2]
	—per share[4]	5.08[2][3]
	Dividends on Common Stock—total	53.8
	—per share[4]	2.45
Balance Sheet Data[5]	Net working capital	272.8
	Ratio of current assets to current liabilities	1.64
	Long-term debt	363.6
	Stockholders' equity	1,117.2

		1966
Gross Property Accounts[5]	Leases	267.7
	Wells and equipment	1,013.8
	Total petroleum production	1,281.5
	Refineries and natural gasoline plants	239.2
	Petroleum marketing	170.8
	Petroleum transportation	148.0
	Coal and related activities	54.8
	Plant foods	161.0
	Chemicals and plastics	117.0
	Other	73.7
	TOTAL GROSS PROPERTY ACCOUNTS	2,246.0
	Per cent of total gross property accounts in United States	80.2

		1966
Capital Expenditures	Petroleum production	112.6
	Refineries and natural gasoline plants	17.5
	Petroleum marketing	29.0
	Petroleum transportation	11.8
	Total petroleum	170.9
	Coal and related activities	54.8
	Plant foods	26.4
	Chemicals and plastics	13.6
	Other	16.7
	TOTAL CAPITAL EXPENDITURES	282.4
	Per cent of total capital expenditures in United States	76.4

		1966
Expenditures For Petroleum Production	Exploratory expense, including land, geological, and geophysical activities	28.6
	Lease rentals	7.3
	Acquisition of new and renewal leases	29.9
	Producing wells and equipment	64.3
	Dry holes	18.4
	TOTAL EXPENDITURES FOR PETROLEUM PRODUCTION	148.5
	Surrendered leases	8.4

	1966
Number of employees[5]	31,959
Number of stockholders—Common[5]	50,796
—Preferred[5][6]	7,641
Shares outstanding—Common (thousands)[4][5]	22,678.1
—Preferred (thousands)[5][6]	2,040.3

[1] The figures in this table are for Continental and consolidated subsidiaries. The American Agricultural Chemical Company, which was acquired in a pooling-of-interests in 1963, has been included commencing in 1957. Companies acquired in pooling transactions in 1959 and 1961 have been included beginning in 1958.

1965	1964	1963	1962	1961	1960	1959	1958	1957
$ 671.0	$ 627.3	$ 583.1	$ 523.7	$ 477.5	$ 449.6	$ 441.7	$ 419.7	$ 342.2
140.5	134.8	126.2	115.6	109.4	103.3	93.8	86.3	68.8
414.5	354.8	322.6	250.4	249.0	250.5	244.4	244.6	243.5
51.2	48.2	42.8	36.0	26.6	25.9	23.8	17.5	15.2
—	—	—	—	—	—	—	—	—
130.0	110.0	95.0	76.1	77.0	71.2	73.3	64.6	59.0
132.3	86.9	64.8	51.9	50.5	49.8	48.9	44.1	37.0
55.5	45.2	51.0	41.4	25.9	22.5	26.4	18.5	12.5
14.6	13.6	15.8	10.8	9.1	8.8	7.4	10.2	10.0
1,609.6	1,420.8	1,301.3	1,105.9	1,025.0	981.6	959.7	905.5	788.2
406.2	357.7	314.9	267.5	270.4	271.5	262.4	263.2	249.6
226.8	228.8	212.4	186.8	171.5	171.3	173.6	152.4	150.3
96.2	100.1	87.4	73.8	68.3	65.8	74.7	65.1	63.8
4.1	4.1	4.1	4.1	4.1	4.1	3.7	3.7	3.7
92.1	96.0	83.3	69.7	64.2	61.7	71.0	61.4	60.1
4.25	4.44	3.88	3.26	3.00	2.89	3.33	3.01	3.06
52.0	45.4	40.7	37.4	36.2	35.8	35.2	31.4	31.4
2.40	2.10	1.90	1.75	1.70	1.70	1.70	1.60	1.60
204.9	191.9	184.7	194.6	194.7	163.0	164.0	177.1	155.0
1.80	1.95	1.96	2.22	2.50	2.18	2.21	2.66	2.80
359.3	324.4	292.5	240.1	247.2	188.1	185.1	205.0	202.6
939.3	898.1	836.3	787.1	756.6	726.6	699.1	604.0	555.2
262.7	253.9	266.3	223.7	213.7	209.8	194.7	146.0	140.1
983.5	942.4	878.7	815.9	768.7	734.2	682.3	628.7	579.2
1,246.2	1,196.3	1,145.0	1,039.6	982.4	944.0	877.0	774.7	719.3
227.5	216.7	207.7	182.9	179.5	164.7	154.7	151.3	131.7
151.0	138.3	127.5	116.9	129.5	114.2	104.2	97.4	86.7
142.8	129.9	112.6	77.0	69.5	62.2	51.5	45.5	45.5
—	—	—	—	—	—	—	—	—
135.3	101.0	84.6	70.1	68.9	62.0	53.2	47.4	41.7
98.1	87.9	45.6	36.9	37.8	30.6	27.2	23.1	15.6
60.5	59.9	57.0	44.1	53.2	46.0	36.3	33.0	32.3
2,061.4	1,930.0	1,780.0	1,567.5	1,520.8	1,423.7	1,304.1	1,172.4	1,072.8
80.3	80.9	81.4	82.7	86.5	87.8	88.0	89.1	89.1
102.3	110.7	143.7	98.3	85.3	116.6	133.9	84.7	129.1
13.9	10.7	26.3	7.1	16.6	10.1	9.2	6.0	8.6
20.9	19.9	18.2	25.7	17.7	17.0	8.5	4.6	11.8
10.3	17.2	29.4	20.7	8.0	3.1	4.5	1.6	3.6
147.4	158.5	217.6	151.8	127.6	146.8	156.1	96.9	153.1
—	—	—	—	—	—	—	—	—
36.3	19.8	13.3	3.2	8.0	10.4	6.8	6.6	5.1
9.4	39.6	6.6	1.4	11.1	6.6	4.4	.9	1.6
6.7	7.1	11.7	4.4	9.1	10.7	3.6	1.9	3.4
199.8	225.0	249.2	160.8	155.8	174.5	170.9	106.3	163.2
73.5	69.5	65.4	62.7	72.9	78.7	77.6	83.3	71.0
30.1	29.1	23.2	27.1	26.0	24.9	21.4	20.8	23.3
7.6	7.1	7.4	8.2	7.9	7.8	6.9	6.6	7.7
22.3	16.3	58.8	24.0	18.9	34.6	52.6	15.0	38.0
60.6	76.5	64.8	55.2	50.5	58.9	62.9	55.7	68.9
19.4	17.9	20.1	19.1	15.9	23.1	18.4	14.0	22.2
140.0	146.9	174.3	133.6	119.2	149.3	162.2	112.1	160.1
12.6	11.5	13.4	12.0	11.4	8.8	9.8	9.1	7.6
21,261	20,022	19,211	18,303	17,110	16,716	16,348	15,874	13,882
38,400	38,715	38,319	39,895	40,104	40,329	37,550	31,017	30,504
7,615	7,739	7,160	10,967	11,350	10,300	9,500	8,100	8,200
21,670.0	21,648.1	21,442.0	21,396.8	21,395.4	21,349.2	21,329.3	20,426.7	19,627.5
2,040.9	2,040.9	2,040.9	2,040.9	2,040.9	2,040.9	1,853.8	1,824.8	1,824.8

(2) Excludes gain (net of related income taxes) of $41.3 million, or $1.88 per Common share, from liquidation of Great Lakes Pipe Line Company in March 1966.
(3) Based on the weighted average number of shares outstanding during the year.
(4) For comparative purposes, the figures for 1957 have been adjusted to reflect the share-for-share distribution made in February 1957.
(5) At December 31.
(6) Pro forma prior to October 21, 1963.

CONTINENTAL OIL COMPANY ANNUAL REPORT 1966

**CONTINENTAL OIL CO.
ANNUAL REPORT 1966**

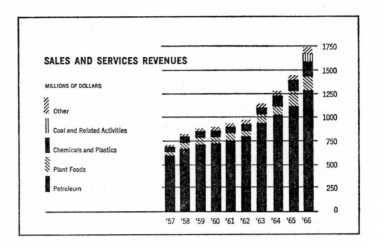

	Per Cent of Total	
	1966	**1965**
Refined products (excluding excise taxes)	44%	46%
Crude oil	27	29
Natural gas	3	4
Coal and related activities	5	—
Plant foods	8	9
Chemicals and plastics	10	9
Other	3	3
Total	100%	100%
Total sales and service revenues (millions of dollars)	$1,749	$1,450

CONTINENTAL OIL COMPANY ANNUAL REPORT 1966

Significant Areas of Undeveloped Acreage

At December 31, 1966

	Net Acres
Anadarko Basin (Oklahoma, Texas, Colorado)	251,000
Delaware Basin (New Mexico, Texas)	188,000
Eastern Platform (Texas)	275,000
Gulf of Mexico (Offshore Louisiana & Texas)	76,000
Powder River Basin (Wyoming, Montana)	324,000
South Texas Cretaceous Area (Texas)	283,000
Sweetgrass Arch (Montana)	119,000
Williston Basin (Montana, North Dakota)	505,000

Discoveries and Extensions

NEW FIELDS

Block 33, Grand Isle Area (Offshore Louisiana)	Oil & Gas
Block 41 E/2, Grand Isle Area (Offshore Louisiana)	Oil & Gas
Block 119, Vermillion Area (Offshore Louisiana)	Oil & Gas
Block 83, East Cameron (Offshore Louisiana)	Gas
Heart River (Stark Co., North Dakota)	Oil
Tinsley (Yazoo Co., Mississippi)	Gas-Condensate
Southwest Sheffield (Pecos Co., Texas)	Oil
Kyle "A" Block (Loving Co., Texas)	Gas-Condensate
Lyons Point (Acadia Parish, Louisiana)	Gas-Condensate

NEW RESERVOIRS AND EXTENSIONS

Block 43, Grand Isle Area (Offshore Louisiana)	Oil & Gas
Block 120, Eugene Island Area (Offshore Louisiana)	Oil
Block 58, West Delta Area (Offshore Louisiana)	Gas-Condensate
Block 22 S/2, South Timbalier Area (Offshore Louisiana)	Oil
Block 64, East Cameron Area (Offshore Louisiana)	Gas
Anadarko Basin (Oklahoma)	Oil & Gas-Condensate

Significant Development Drilling Activity

	Type Of Well	Producing Wells Completed in 1966 Gross	Net
Chittim Anticline (Southwest Texas)	Oil	178	178.0
San Juan Basin (Northwest New Mexico)	Gas	135	54.0
Gulf Coast Salt Dome (Offshore Louisiana)	Oil & Gas	70	18.3
Powder River Basin (Central Wyoming)	Oil	48	4.8
Central Basin Platform (West Texas & Southeast New Mexico)	Oil & Gas	28	10.7
Jackson & Frio Trend Areas (South Texas)	Oil & Gas	24	11.7
Anadarko Basin (West Oklahoma)	Oil & Gas	20	4.5
Santa Maria Province (California)	Oil	12	12.0
North Central Oklahoma Platform	Oil & Gas	8	6.2
Midland Basin (West Texas)	Oil	7	6.9

Drilling Program

	Gross Wells		Net Wells	
	1966	1965	1966	1965
EXPLORATORY WELLS				
Oil	9	9	4	6
Gas	8	10	3	6
Dry	49	75	31	42
	66	94	38	54
DEVELOPMENT WELLS				
Oil	431	384	261	167
Gas	209	136	78	56
Dry	71	73	38	36
	711	593	377	259
TOTAL	777	687	415	313

Changes in Net Crude Oil and Condensate Production

	Barrels Daily		
	1966	1965	% Change
PRORATED STATES			
Louisiana — Offshore	19,226	15,881	21.1
Oklahoma	10,289	9,710	6.0
Texas	46,064	43,874	5.0
New Mexico	9,647	9,531	1.2
Other	15,905	16,674	(4.6)
	101,131	95,670	5.7
NONPRORATED STATES			
Illinois	1,683	1,484	13.4
California	7,481	7,721	(3.1)
Wyoming	37,885	40,902	(7.4)
Utah	1,586	1,870	(15.1)
Colorado	1,785	2,168	(17.7)
Other	6,097	6,278	(2.9)
	56,517	60,423	(6.5)
TOTAL	157,648	156,093	1.0

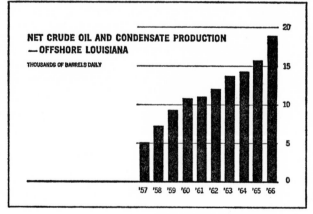

NET CRUDE OIL AND CONDENSATE PRODUCTION — OFFSHORE LOUISIANA

THOUSANDS OF BARRELS DAILY

'57 '58 '59 '60 '61 '62 '63 '64 '65 '66

NET CRUDE OIL AND CONDENSATE PRODUCTION

THOUSANDS OF BARRELS DAILY

Canada

United States

(Bar chart showing years '57 '58 '59 '60 '61 '62 '63 '64 '65 '66 with scale 0, 50, 100, 150, 200)

Sales of Refined Products

PRODUCT	Barrels Daily		% Change
	1966	1965	
Motor gasoline	114,807	106,556	7.7%
Other gasoline	24,462	27,602	(11.4)
Commercial jet fuel	11,101	8,848	25.5
Other kerosene and distillate	82,506	73,085	12.9
LPG and natural gasoline	34,402	33,089	4.0
Asphalt and residual fuel oil	33,446	28,909	15.7
Lubricating oil	5,744	4,793	19.8
Other products	6,690	7,021	(4.7)
TOTAL	313,158	289,903	8.0%

Undeveloped Net Acreage Holdings

At December 31, 1966

Thousands of Acres

LOCATION	Crown permits or Reservations*	Leaseholds	Options to Lease Hudson's Bay Company Lands	Fee Lands	Total
Alberta	2,944	1,887	1,519	84	6,434
British Columbia	567	452	6	—	1,025
Saskatchewan	2,686	85	2,324	101	5,196
Yukon and Northwest Territories	2,033	—	—	—	2,033
Maritime Provinces	9,167	—	—	—	9,167
Other	—	—	700	89	789
TOTAL	17,397	2,424	4,549	274	24,644

*Convertible into leases to the extent of approximately 50%.

Discoveries and Extensions

NEW FIELDS
Zama Lake Area (Alberta)..Oil & Gas
Hummingbird Area (Saskatchewan)...Oil
Beatty Lake Area (Alberta)..Oil

NEW RESERVOIRS AND EXTENSIONS
Brazeau River Area (Alberta)..Gas
Kaybob South Area (Alberta)..Gas-Condensate
Clarke Lake Area (British Columbia)...Gas

Drilling Program

	Gross Wells		Net Wells	
	1966	1965	1966	1965
EXPLORATORY WELLS				
Oil	14	12	9	7
Gas	14	8	9	4
Dry	75	49	40	29
	103	69	58	40
DEVELOPMENT WELLS				
Oil	60	74	35	39
Gas	37	31	10	10
Dry	22	21	12	11
	119	126	57	60
TOTAL	222	195	115	100

Changes in Net Crude Oil Production

	Barrels Daily		
PROVINCE	1966	1965	% Change
Alberta	25,856	25,456	1.6
British Columbia	5,247	3,083	70.2
Saskatchewan	4,826	4,582	5.3
Manitoba	14	13	7.7
TOTAL	35,943	33,134	8.5

Undeveloped Acreage Holdings

At December 31, 1966

	Thousands	
	Gross Acres	Net Acres
EASTERN HEMISPHERE		
Africa		
Libya	24,437	8,295
Tunisia	4,683	1,561
Middle East		
Bahrain	880	440
Dhofar	19,200	6,400
Dubai	1,756	797
Iran	3,127	262
Qatar	5,694	2,847
Turkey	494	213
Europe		
Germany	914	294
United Kingdom	4,648	1,118
Asia-Pacific		
Australia	129,185	36,358
Papua-New Guinea	24,544	12,182
OTHER WESTERN HEMISPHERE		
Guyana	10,256	5,128
TOTAL	229,818	75,895

Drilling Program

	Gross Wells		Net Wells	
	1966	1965	1966	1965
Oil	6	50	2	17
Dry	19	28	6	11
TOTAL	25	78	8	28

Sales and approximate earnings by markets served were as follows:

	1966 (Amounts in Millions)			
	SALES		EARNINGS	
	Amount	% of Total	Amount	% of Total
Products for the Home	$ 672.5	64%	$29.4	62%
Products for Industry	217.4	21	8.3	18
Products for Business	159.3	15	9.6	20
TOTAL	$1,049.2	100%	$47.3	100%

Sales increased 7.1 per cent over 1965 with improvement in all markets served:

	1966	1965	CHANGE
	(Amounts in Millions)		
Products for the Home	$ 672.5	$642.8	+ 4.6%
Products for Industry	217.4	198.7	+ 9.4
Products for Business	159.3	138.3	+15.2
TOTAL	$1,049.2	$979.8	+ 7.1%

U.S. sales accounted for 48.7 per cent of the total in 1966, increasing at a faster rate than foreign sales. Sales by major geographical areas were as follows:

	1966	1965	CHANGE
	(Amounts in Millions)		
United States	$ 510.7	$470.3	+ 8.6%
Europe	248.4	237.1	+ 4.8
Latin America	124.4	110.6	+12.5
Far East	82.9	87.5	− 5.3
Africa and the Near East	50.1	46.1	+ 8.7
Canada	32.7	28.2	+16.0
TOTAL	$1,049.2	$979.8	+ 7.1%

In addition to household sewing machines and related products, principal consumer products include home entertainment equipment, refrigerators, washing machines, portable electric hand tools, floor-care equipment, knitting machines, kitchen ranges, typewriters and wood products.

Sales of products for the home by major categories were as follows:

	1966	1965	CHANGE
	(Amounts in Millions)		
Sewing machines	$471.7	$454.9	+ 3.7%
Major appliances	72.9	58.5	+24.6
Home entertainment equipment	67.3	64.6	+ 4.2
Other	60.6	64.8	− 6.5
TOTAL	$672.5	$642.8	+ 4.6%

Sales of products for the home by major geographical areas were as follows:

	1966	1965	CHANGE
	(Amounts in Millions)		
United States	$244.4	$234.4	+ 4.3%
Europe	182.9	176.1	+ 3.9
Latin America	111.2	94.7	+17.4
Far East	69.4	75.2	− 7.7
Africa and the Near East	44.5	41.3	+ 7.7
Canada	20.1	21.1	− 4.7
TOTAL	$672.5	$642.8	+ 4.6%

Major industrial products and services are industrial sewing machines and allied equipment, heating and air conditioning, tufting, knitting and other textile machinery, instrumentation, information systems, industrial controls and special purpose electric motors.

Sales of industrial products by major product categories were as follows:

	1966	1965	CHANGE
	(Amounts in Millions)		
Industrial sewing equipment..	$88.8	$79.9	+11.1%
Heating and air conditioning..	31.7	24.6	+28.9
Textile machinery	29.4	33.9	−13.3
Instrumentation	25.8	23.4	+10.3
Information systems	23.2	19.1	+21.5
Other	18.5	17.8	+ 3.9
TOTAL	$217.4	$198.7	+ 9.4%

Sales of products and services for industry by major geographical areas were as follows:

	1966	1965	CHANGE
	(Amounts in Millions)		
United States	$155.7	$139.4	+11.7%
Europe	34.6	32.2	+ 7.5
Other	27.1	27.1	—
TOTAL	$217.4	$198.7	+ 9.4%

Systems equipment, calculators, graphic arts equipment, adding machines, postage meters and mailing equipment are our principal products for business. Virtually all business equipment produced and sold by the Company bears the Friden trademark.

Sales of products and services for business by major categories were as follows:

	1966	1965	CHANGE
	(Amounts in Millions)		
Systems equipment	$ 60.8	$ 57.1	+ 6.5%
Calculators and adding machines	47.0	40.8	+15.2
Repairs and services	31.6	27.9	+13.3
Other	19.9	12.5	+59.2
TOTAL	$159.3	$138.3	+15.2%

Sales of products for business by major geographical areas were as follows:

	1966	1965	CHANGE
	(Amounts in Millions)		
United States	$110.6	$ 96.5	+14.6%
Europe	30.9	28.8	+ 7.3
Other	17.8	13.0	+36.9
TOTAL	$159.3	$138.3	+15.2%

NET SALES

Sales in 1966 totaled a record $1,049.2 million, and were $69.4 million or 7.1 per cent higher than 1965 net sales.

Sales of our traditional products, household and industrial sewing machines and related items, amounted to $560.5 million in 1966 and were 53.5 per cent of the total. In 1965, sales of such products were $534.8 million or 54.6 per cent of the total.

Sales of other products, which comprised 46.5 per cent of the total, were $488.7 million. This was an increase of 9.8 per cent over 1965 sales of $445.0 million.

In 1966, foreign sales were 51.3 per cent of the total, compared with 52.0 per cent in 1965. Sales in the United States increased 8.6 per cent while foreign sales increased 5.7 per cent.

Sales by major geographical area are shown in the following table:

	1966		1965	
	(Amounts in Millions)			
	Amount	% of Total	Amount	% of Total
United States	$ 510.7	48.7%	$470.3	48.0%
Europe	248.4	23.7	237.1	24.2
Latin America	124.4	11.8	110.6	11.3
Far East	82.9	7.9	87.5	8.9
Africa and the Near East	50.1	4.8	46.1	4.7
Canada	32.7	3.1	28.2	2.9
	$1,049.2	100.0%	$979.8	100.0%

OTHER ASSETS

Other assets at December 31, 1966 and 1965 were as follows:

	1966	1965
	(Amounts in Millions)	
Prepaid expenses and deferred charges	$ 19.1	$ 15.5
Mortgages and other	14.0	12.6
Intangibles, less amortization	9.6	10.2
Deposits	5.7	7.6
	$ 48.4	$ 45.9

FOREIGN NET ASSETS

Net assets located outside the United States are expressed in U.S. dollars at appropriate exchange rates. Foreign net assets at December 31, 1966 and 1965 by major geographical area were:

	1966	1965
	(Amounts in Millions)	
Europe	$134.3	$124.4
Latin America	82.7	66.9
Far East	44.0	49.2
Africa and the Near East	29.8	24.9
Canada	17.7	16.8
	$308.5	$282.2

THE SINGER COMPANY ANNUAL REPORT 1966

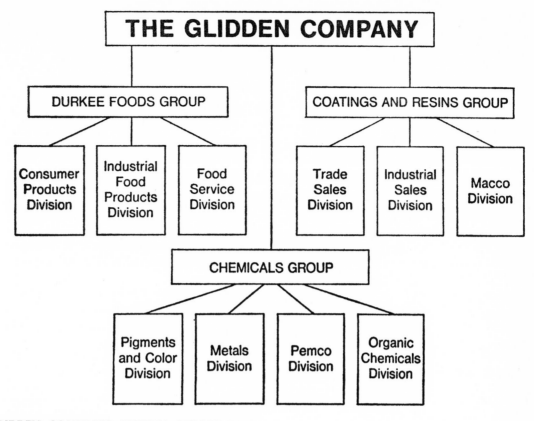

THE GLIDDEN COMPANY

DURKEE FOODS GROUP

Consumer Products Division

Industrial Food Products Division

Food Service Division

COATINGS AND RESINS GROUP

Trade Sales Division

Industrial Sales Division

Macco Division

CHEMICALS GROUP

Pigments and Color Division

Metals Division

Pemco Division

Organic Chemicals Division

THE GLIDDEN COMPANY ANNUAL REPORT 1966

Coatings and Resins Group

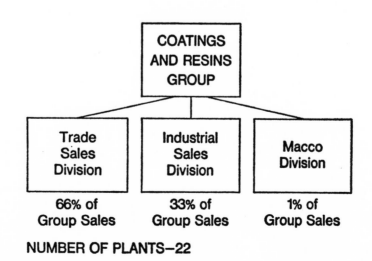

COATINGS AND RESINS GROUP

Trade Sales Division

Industrial Sales Division

Macco Division

66% of Group Sales

33% of Group Sales

1% of Group Sales

NUMBER OF PLANTS—22

Durkee Foods Group

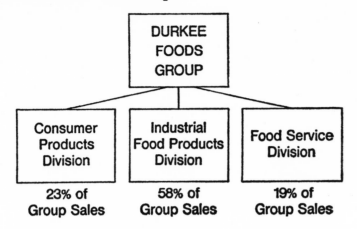

DURKEE
FOODS
GROUP

Consumer Products Division	Industrial Food Products Division	Food Service Division
23% of Group Sales	58% of Group Sales	19% of Group Sales

NUMBER OF PLANTS—15

**THE GLIDDEN COMPANY
ANNUAL REPORT 1966**

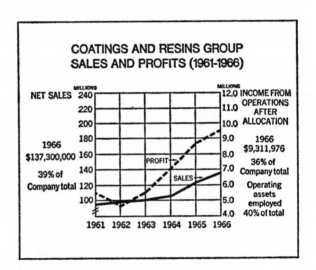

COATINGS AND RESINS GROUP
SALES AND PROFITS (1961-1966)

NET SALES

1966
$137,300,000

39% of
Company total

INCOME FROM
OPERATIONS
AFTER
ALLOCATION

1966
$9,311,976

36% of
Company total

Operating
assets
employed
40% of total

PROFIT

SALES

1961 1962 1963 1964 1965 1966

Chemicals Group

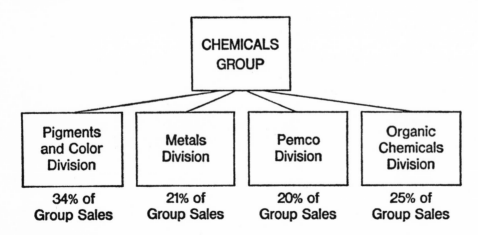

CHEMICALS
GROUP

Pigments and Color Division	Metals Division	Pemco Division	Organic Chemicals Division
34% of Group Sales	21% of Group Sales	20% of Group Sales	25% of Group Sales

NUMBER OF PLANTS—9

DISTRIBUTION OF TITANIUM DIOXIDE INDUSTRY SALES

PAINT	56%
PAPER	15%
FLOOR COVERINGS	5%
RUBBER	4%
OTHER	20%
	TOTAL 100%

Sales

Consolidated sales of The Glidden Company were $351,888,467 in fiscal 1966, compared with $303,991,184 in 1965. Sales by operating groups were:

	1966 (000)	1965 (000)	Change
Durkee Foods	$154,500	$126,700	+22%
Coatings & Resins	137,300	121,800	+13%
Chemicals	60,100	55,500	+ 8%
	$351,900	$304,000	

Sales and Profits

Following is the amount and percentage of income from operations after allocating corporate items on the basis of assets employed, along with the percentage of sales and total assets of each operating group in 1966.

	Profit	Profit %	Sales %	Assets %
Durkee Foods	$ 7,844,410	30	44	32
Coatings & Resins	9,311,976	36	39	40
Chemicals	8,690,664	34	17	28
Income from Operations	$25,847,050	100%	100%	100%

Capital Expenditures

Capital expenditures in fiscal 1966 amounted to $11,685,824, compared with $9,866,067 for the previous fiscal year. Here is how capital was invested in the operating groups during the year:

Durkee Foods	30%
Coatings and Resins	47%
Chemicals	23%

137

NATIONAL DISTILLERS AND CHEMICAL CORPORATION

Results in Brief

	% Change 1966-65	1966	1965	1964
Net sales	+8	$898,312,000	$829,031,000	$810,941,000
Net income	+30	$40,680,000	$31,285,000	$27,127,000
Net earnings per common share, after preferred dividends	+30	$3.09	$2.37	$2.02
Cash dividends on common stock—per share*	+14	$1.60	$1.40	$1.20
Funds provided by operations	+9	$56,577,000	$51,907,000	$49,054,000
Book value per common share	+3	$29.28	$28.34	$27.40
Holders of common stock		73,864	74,238	73,578
Employees		14,601	13,615	13,835

*The quarterly dividend on the common stock was increased to 45 cents per share in January 1967.

Divisional Operating Results

Divisions	Net Sales (000 omitted)			Operating Profit (000 omitted)		
	1966	1965	1964	1966	1965	1964
Liquor	$497,474	$469,828	$430,471	$46,840	$45,763	$39,467
Chemicals	133,432	135,952	137,554	24,216	16,444	14,633
Metals	235,095	193,677	216,962	19,933	10,486	5,923
International	11,696	10,924	9,841	2,553	966	28
H. W. Loud Co.	20,615	18,650	16,113	76	1,213	963
Totals	$898,312	$829,031	$810,941	$88,512	$70,514	$59,032

NOTE: Sales of 50 per cent owned domestic affiliates are not included in consolidated net sales; however, the Company's share of net earnings of these affiliates, including Reactive Metals, Inc., is allocated to the Chemical Division.

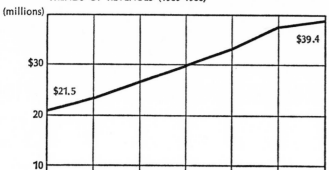

TRENDS OF REVENUES (1960-1966)

(millions)

$30

$21.5

20

$39.4

10

Greyhound Package Express

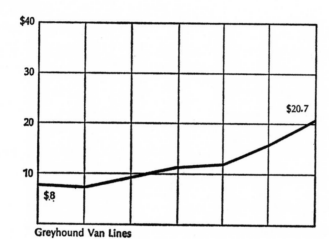

$40

30

20

$20.7

10

$.8

Greyhound Van Lines

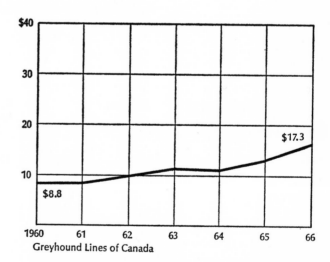

$40

30

20

$17.3

10

$8.8

1960   61   62   63   64   65   66

Greyhound Lines of Canada

Revenue trends were decidedly upward in 1966 in these three
transportation service areas of your company. Greyhound Package
Express—the 24-hour, 7-day-a-week package-shipment service—
continued its dramatic rise. Its revenues climbed from $21.5 million
in 1960 to $39.4 million last year, an 83.6 per cent increase.
Revenues of Greyhound Van Lines, our moving and storage
subsidiary, rose 157.9 per cent—from $8 million in 1960 to $20.7
million last year. And Greyhound Lines of Canada, another rapidly
growing phase of your company, reported 1966 revenues of
$17.3 million, up 96.6 per cent from $8.8 million in 1960.

139

The Greyhound Corporation and Consolidated Subsidiaries

Consolidated Income Statement

	Year ended December 31	
	1966	1965
REVENUES:		
Transportation:		
Passenger	$305,381,786	$297,447,148
Package express	39,371,952	38,081,819
Charter and other	29,543,886	27,994,543
Household moving and storage	20,746,029	15,970,082
Sightseeing, tours and bus manufacturing...	9,708,498	7,636,386
	$404,752,151	$387,129,978
Food services	115,777,115	105,118,213
Insurance	11,974,234	10,438,319
Money orders	6,339,526	5,919,589
Dividends and interest	7,052,642	4,689,801
	$545,895,668	$513,295,900
EXPENSES AND MINORITY INTERESTS:		
Operating costs and expenses	$444,915,643	$414,934,189
Depreciation	21,517,329	20,979,672
Interest	4,913,197	3,230,996
Net income applicable to minority interests...	1,240,732	985,776
	$472,586,901	$440,130,633
INCOME BEFORE INCOME TAXES	$ 73,308,767	$ 73,165,267
PROVISION FOR INCOME TAXES	32,802,000	33,863,000
NET INCOME OF THE CORPORATION AND CONSOLIDATED SUBSIDIARIES	$ 40,506,767	$ 39,302,267
NET INCOME OF GREYHOUND LEASING & FINANCIAL CORPORATION AND SUBSIDIARIES (Note A)	6,216,415	4,127,068
NET INCOME FOR THE YEAR	$ 46,723,182	$ 43,429,335
Net income per share of common stock....	$1.49	$1.38

See notes to financial statements.

Highlights of Ten Years

STATISTICS IN BRIEF (Dollar data in millions)	1966	1965	1964	1963	1962	1961	1960	1959	1958	1957
REVENUES										
Transportation Services	$404.7	387.1	365.3	349.8	334.4	311.2	302.4	297.9	283.2	273.7
Food Services (2)	$115.8	105.1	94.8	82.8	73.3	59.2	56.2	23.8	22.0	21.7
Financial Services and Other (2)	$ 25.4	21.1	8.2	6.9	6.2	5.3	5.2	1.6	.6	1.2
Total	$545.9	513.3	468.3	439.5	413.9	375.7	363.8	323.3	305.8	296.6
NET INCOME										
Total Dollars (2)	$ 46.7	43.4	38.7	34.3	30.2	23.6	22.7	21.4	14.0	13.4
Per Common Share After Preferred Dividends (1)	$ 1.49	1.38	1.23	1.10	.97	.75	.72	.75	.49	.48
PREFERRED DIVIDEND REQUIREMENTS	$ .5	.5	.6	.8	1.3	1.4	1.5	.4	.5	.4
COMMON DIVIDENDS										
Cash	$ 28.0	27.2	22.1	18.7	14.7	13.9	11.9	11.3	10.8	10.6
Per Share, as Adjusted for Stock Dividends and 1964 2-for-1 Stock Split	$ .90	.875	.725	.645	.515	.49	.425	.405	.395	.395
Stock				5%	5%		10%	5%		
TAXES (2)										
Income	$ 32.8	33.9	31.3	35.3	32.7	24.9	24.3	25.0	15.1	14.4
Other	$ 34.3	30.8	29.2	28.1	27.6	26.6	26.1	23.7	23.6	23.6
Total—Per Common Share	$ 2.10	2.04	1.91	2.05	1.99	1.71	1.68	1.71	1.36	1.36
OTHER STATISTICS										
Number of Stockholders	124,784	115,168	103,705	87,141	84,830	83,664	82,508	79,778	76,057	73,103
Number of Employees (Average)	33,930	32,422	31,807	24,264	24,191	24,236	24,387	24,775	26,542	28,140
Miles of Routes	102,181	100,944	100,434	100,302	101,731	101,068	100,433	101,120	101,711	99,896
Bus Miles Operated (Millions)	535.1	526.1	528.4	513.9	508.0	489.5	481.5	485.5	496.4	517.7
Miles Traveled by Passengers (Billions)	10.7	10.3	10.4	10.2	10.1	9.2	9.3	9.5	9.8	10.1
Buses Owned End of Year	5,422	5,216	5,293	5,171	5,324	5,200	5,214	5,383	5,595	5,931

Per share statistics are based on average number of common shares outstanding.
(1) Earnings per common share for all years have been restated for 1964 stock split and for stock dividends.
Net income of companies acquired under pooling principle included for years 1960 to 1965.
(2) Includes acquired companies years 1960 to 1965 under pooling principle.

Public Reporting by Conglomerates—
Recent Developments in the
United Kingdom and Australia

UNITED KINGDOM

The Stock Exchange of London

In August 1964, a letter from Lord Ritchie, Chairman of The Stock Exchange, was circulated among the chairmen of quoted companies. It began,

> I feel sure that you will have noticed in recent years a growing volume of comment and public discussion as to the amount of information being made available by public companies to their shareholders.

Lord Ritchie alluded not only to the 1962 Report of the Company Law Committee (the Jenkins Report), which had been ignored by Parliament, but also the public debates following the Rolls Razor scandal and other financial embarrassments. The dual purpose of Lord Ritchie's letter was to ask quoted companies to consider expanding their disclosures to shareholders, and to announce that the Council of The Stock Exchange proposed to require certain additional disclosures of companies seeking quotation in the future. Among the specific types of disclosure in which The Stock Exchange expressed particular interest was the following item:

> where a company or group carries on widely differing operations, the provision of an analysis of trading results [is desirable]; . . . .

Attached to the letter was an Appendix in which the recommendations were given in greater detail, including the following amplification:

> Sales turnover figures should be included in the report, together with a breakdown between the more important trading divisions. . . . In certain cases it is advisable to split turnover geographically or between products.

As to the part of the letter recommending new types of disclosure to quoted companies, The Stock Exchange reported two-and-a-half years later that the response was, in the main, very good, the majority of companies having been most cooperative. In regard to newly quoted companies, The Stock Exchange promulgated a "supplemental undertaking" effective for applications on and after March 26, 1965, which required applicants to agree to supply, *inter alia*, the following additional disclosure:

> To include in or circulate with each annual Directors' Report [equivalent to the President's Letter in the United States] and Audited Accounts or Chairman's Statement:—
>
> (a)(1) A description of the operations carried on by the Company or, if the company has subsidiaries, the Group.
>
> (2) If the Company or, as the case may be, the Group carries on widely differing operations, a statement showing the contributions [in figures or percentages] of such respective differing operations to its trading results.
>
> (3) If the Company or, as the case may be, the Group trades outside the United Kingdom, a statement showing a geographical analysis [in figures or percentages] of its trading operations.

The terms "trading results" and "trading operations" were not defined by The Stock Exchange.

The same paragraphs were later incorporated in The Stock Exchange's General Undertaking (i.e., listing agreement) for companies seeking quotation after August 31, 1966.

When companies not previously quoted issue a prospectus covering securities that are to be quoted, The Stock Exchange now expects the following types of disclosure:

> 15. The general nature of the business of the Company or Group and, in cases where the Company or Group carries on two or more activities which are material, having regard to profits or losses, assets employed or any other factors, information as to the relative importance of each such activity. If the Company or Group trades outside the United Kingdom a statement showing a geographical analysis of its trading operations.
>
>   ❋   ❋   ❋
>
> 17. Wherever possible, a statement showing the sales turnover figures or gross trading income during the preceding three financial years which should contain a reasonable breakdown between the more important trading activities. . . .[1]

Again, key terms are not defined.

Companies Act 1967   On February 2, 1966, the Labor Government introduced a Companies Bill in the House of Commons, which provided, in Clause 15, that com-

---

[1] *Admission of Securities to Quotation*, Memoranda of Guidance and Requirements of the Federation of Stock Exchanges in Great Britain and Ireland; June 1966; p. 66.

panies carrying on "business of two or more classes that differ substantially from each other" shall disclose in the directors' report

(a) the proportions in which the turnover [i.e., sales] for that year . . . is divided amongst those classes; and

(b) as regards business of each class, the extent or appropriate extent (expressed, in either case, in monetary terms) to which, in the opinion of the directors, the carrying on of business of that class contributed to, or restricted, the profit or loss of the company for that year before taxation.

Parliament later adjourned without acting on the Bill; however, a Companies Bill with a virtually identical clause (but numbered 17) was presented in the House of Lords on November 3, 1966. While the new Companies Bill was being considered by Parliament, The Institute of Chartered Accountants in England and Wales, The Institute of Chartered Accountants of Scotland, and The Association of Certified and Corporate Accountants submitted a joint memorandum on the Bill to the President of the Board of Trade. In regard to Clause 17, which was located in the section of the Bill on "directors' reports" and not in the section dealing with information covered by the auditor's opinion, the joint memorandum said:

> The accountancy bodies consider that the analysis required by clause 17 should be made a statement "annexed" to the accounts and thus removed from the directors' report. The requirement will confront many companies with difficult problems of interpretation, allocation and presentation to which the answers will be matters of opinion involving, perhaps extensively, the exercise of judgment. This, however, is a feature of many problems which already arise in drawing up accounts. Moreover the information called for is accounting information which may itself be highly relevant to the presentation of a true and fair view of the results of the year. For these reasons it seems proper that the opinion of the directors as expressed in the information which is given should be subjected to the judgment of the auditors.[2]

The proposal was apparently never seriously considered by Parliament, which, indeed, accepted a Board of Trade amendment that softened the disclosure requirement. In the closing days of debate in Commons, Mr. George Darling, Minister of State (Board of Trade), successfully amended Clause 17 to give explicitly to the directors the discretion to determine whether the two or more classes of business "differ substantially from each other"—a determination for which the Companies Bill offered no guidelines at all. Clause 17, as amended, became law when the Companies Act 1967 received Royal Assent on July 27, 1967. By special provision in the Act,

---

[2] "The Companies Bill: Joint Memorandum to Board of Trade," *The Acountant*, January 28, 1967, p. 111.

the effective date of Clause 17 is delayed one year; it will apply to financial years ending on and after July 27, 1968. The final version of Clause 17 is as follows:

17.—(1) If, in the course of a financial year, a company (being one subject to the requirements of paragraph 13A of Schedule 8 to the principal Act but not being one that has subsidiaries at the end of that year and submits in respect of that year group accounts prepared as consolidated accounts) has carried on business of two or more classes (other than banking or discounting or a class prescribed for the purposes of sub-paragraph (2) of that paragraph) that, in the opinion of the directors, differ substantially from each other, there shall be contained in the director's report relating to that year a statement of—

(a) the proportions in which the turnover for that year (so far as stated in the accounts in respect of that year in pursuance of that Schedule) is divided amongst those classes (describing them); and

(b) as regards business of each class, the extent or approximate extent (expressed, in either case, in monetary terms) to which, in the opinion of the directors, the carrying on of business of that class contributed to, or restricted, the profit or loss of the company for that year before taxation.

(2) If—

(a) a company has subsidiaries at the end of its financial year and submits in respect of that year group accounts prepared as consolidated accounts; and

(b) the company and the subsidiaries dealt with by the accounts carried on between them in the course of the year business of two or more classes (other than banking or discounting or a class prescribed for the purposes of paragraph 13A(2) of Schedule 8 to the principal Act) that, in the opinion of the directors, differ substantially from each other;

there shall be contained in the directors' report relating to that year a statement of—

(i) the proportions in which the turnover for that year (so far as stated in the accounts in respect of that year in pursuance of that Schedule) is divided amongst those classes (describing them); and

(ii) as regards business of each class, the extent or approximate extent (expressed, in either case, in monetary terms) to which, in the opinion of the directors of the company, the carrying on of business of that class contributed to, or restricted, the profit or loss for that year (before taxation) of the company and the subsidiaries dealt with by the accounts.

(3) For the purposes of this section, classes of business which, in the opinion of the directors, do not differ substantially from each other shall be treated as one class.

As has been customary with Company Law in the United Kingdom, novel disclosure provisions are stated at first somewhat cautiously, allowing a period of experimentation. This reason was cited by the Board of Trade for giving directors the explicit authority to decide whether their two or more classes of business "differ substantially from each other."

AUSTRALIA

A recent development in Australia might be introduced for contrast. Effective November 1, 1967, the listing manual of the Australian Associated Stock Exchanges was amended to require published accounts to contain the names of consolidated subsidiaries which incurred losses, together with information on the extent of such losses. The listing manual was also amended to recommend, but not require, public disclosure of "net trading results" and provisions for depreciation and taxation and "final net profit" of each subsidiary.[3]

While the breakdown of financial information in the United Kingdom has pertained to classes of business that differ substantially (or widely) from each other, in Australia it has so far been limited to subsidiaries.

SELECTED BIBLIOGRAPHY ON THE COMPANIES ACT 1967

The Companies Act 1967, Some Requirements and Implications, Edinburgh: Published by the Accountants' Publishing Co. Ltd. for The Institute of Chartered Accountants of Scotland, 1967, 100 pp.

Frank H. Jones, *Supplement to "Guide to Company Balance Sheets & Profit and Loss Accounts,"* Cambridge: W. Heffer and Sons Ltd., 1967, 64 pp.

Guide to the Accounting Requirements of The Companies Acts 1948–1967, London: Published for the General Educational Trust of The Institute of Chartered Accountants in England and Wales by Gee & Co. (Publishers) Limited, 1967, 36 pp.

[3] L. Foldes, "1967 Amendments to the Official Listing Requirements of the Australian Associated Stock Exchanges," *The Chartered Accountant in Australia*, October 1967, pp. 329, 331.

Participants

Anderson, Corliss D.
Financial Analyst
Barrington, Illinois

Backer, Morton
Professor of Accounting
School of Business Administration
University of Massachusetts
Amherst, Massachusetts

Barr, Andrew
Chief Accountant
Securities and Exchange Commission
Washington, D. C.

Bevis, Donald J., Partner
Touche, Ross, Bailey & Smart
New York, New York

Blair, John M.
Chief Economist
Senate Anti-Trust and Monopoly Sub-
    committee
Washington, D. C.

Bows, Albert J., Partner
Arthur Andersen & Company
Atlanta, Georgia

Browne, D. E.
Group Vice President-Finance and Ad-
    ministration
Lockheed Aircraft Corporation
Burbank, California

Browne, Donald
Vice President and Treasurer
Kaiser Industries Corporation
Oakland, California

Bubul, Joseph L., Partner
Ernst & Ernst
St. Louis, Missouri

Campbell, Don H.
Assistant Controller
Tenneco Inc.
Houston, Texas

Chetkovich, Michael N., Partner
Haskins & Sells
New York, New York

Daniels, Edwin C., Partner
Ernst & Ernst
New Orleans, Louisiana

Davidson, Sidney
Arthur Young Professor of Accounting
Graduate School of Business
University of Chicago
Chicago, Illinois

Dirlam, Joel B.
Professor of Economics
College of Business Administration
University of Rhode Island
Kingston, Rhode Island

Flaherty, John J.
Analyst, Staff Accounting Dept.

Finance Staff
Ford Motor Company
Dearborn, Michigan

Flint, Robert N.
Assistant Comptroller
American Telephone and Telegraph
  Company
New York, New York

Hall, David F.
American Telephone and Telegraph
  Company
New York, New York

Hall, William D., Partner
Arthur Andersen & Co.
Chicago, Illinois

Halvorson, Newman T., Partner
Ernst & Ernst
Cleveland, Ohio

Harrison, William H.
Vice President and Controller
General Telephone and Electronics
  Corporation
New York, New York

Hartmann, John J.
Vice President
Kern County Land Company
San Francisco, California

Heath, Loyd
Accounting Research Division
American Institute of CPA's
New York, New York

Henderson, G. D.
General Commercial Manager for Lou-
  isiana
American Telephone and Telegraph
  Company
New Orleans, Louisiana

Hopkins, E. Wayne
Vice President
Tenneco Inc.
Houston, Texas

Hughes, Roy E.
Vice President and Controller
Kaiser Industries Corporation
Oakland, California

Lynch, Thomas M., Partner
Ernst & Ernst
Cleveland, Ohio

MacCallan, W. D.
Vice President, Research
The Adams Express Company
New York, New York

Makela, Benjamin R., Research
  Director
Financial Executives Research
  Foundation Inc.
New York, New York

Mandell, David
Supervisor, Staff Accounting Dept.
Finance Staff
Ford Motor Company
Dearborn, Michigan

Mautz, R. K.
Professor, College of Commerce and
  Business Administration
Department of Accountancy
University of Illinois
Urbana, Illinois

McFarland, Walter B., Director of Re-
  search
National Association of Accountants
New York, New York

McInnes, Allen T.
Director of Financial Planning
Tenneco Inc.
Houston, Texas

Nabi, Stanley A., Partner—Research
Schweickart & Company
New York, New York

Parker, C. Reed, Vice President
Duff, Anderson & Clark, Inc.
Chicago, Illinois

Peck, E. Stanley, Jr.
Director of Operations,
  Securities Division
American Stock Exchange
New York, New York

Pfenning, Robert E.
Comptroller
General Electric Company
New York, New York

Sentilles, I. F., Partner
Peat, Marwick, Mitchell & Co.
Dallas, Texas

Solomons, David
Professor of Accounting
Wharton School of Finance and
  Commerce
University of Pennsylvania
Philadelphia, Penn.

Sommer, A. A., Jr., Partner
Calfee, Halter, Calfee, Griswold and
  Sommer
Cleveland, Ohio

Vaughn, E. A.
Vice President and Controller
Alcoa Foundation
Pittsburgh, Pennsylvania

Wear, Allan
Manager, Staff Accounting Dept.
Finance Staff
Ford Motor Company
Dearborn, Michigan

Weston, J. Fred
Chairman, Business Economics and
  Finance
Graduate School of Business Admin.
University of California
Los Angeles, California

White, Zach T., Partner
Price Waterhouse & Co.
New York, New York

Wick, Merle S.
Vice President
New York Stock Exchange
New York, New York

Wilson, Alfred M.
Executive Vice President
Honeywell Inc.
Minneapolis, Minn.

Chronological Bibliography on Conglomerate Reporting

1. Cohen, Manuel F., "Analysts, Accountants and the SEC—Necessary Joint Efforts," address before the Nineteenth Annual Conference of the Financial Analysts Federation, New York City, May 24, 1966; printed in *The Journal of Accountancy* (August, 1966), 57–62.

2. Anonymous letters to the editor in the *Financial Executive* (June, 1966), 4–8, and (October, 1966), 4–7.

3. "Next: Divisional Profit Reporting by Public Corporations," *Forbes* (July 15, 1966), 16–17.

4. Testimony and exhibits of George M. Bunker and Manuel F. Cohen, *Economic Concentration*, Hearings before the Subcommittee on Anti-Trust and Monopoly of the Committee on the Judiciary, United States Senate, Eighty-Ninth Congress, Second Session, September 19, 20, 1966, Part 5, "Concentration and Divisional Reporting," pp. 1968–1997, 2084–2152.

5. "Conglomerate Companies and Product-Line Disclosure," Editorial in *The Journal of Accountancy* (October, 1966), 33–34.

6. Cohen, Manuel F., "The SEC and Accountants: Co-operative Efforts to Improve Financial Reporting," address before the 79th annual meeting of the American Institute of Certified Public Accountants, Boston, October 5, 1966; printed in *The Journal of Accountancy* (December, 1966), 56–60.

7. Bows, Albert J., Jr., "Problems in Disclosure of Segments of Conglomerate Companies," *The Journal of Accountancy* (December, 1966), 33–37.

8. Lanterman, Joseph B., "How to Resolve the Financial Reporting Controversy," *Financial Executive* (December, 1966), 40–48.

9. Loomis, Carol J., "Where Manny Cohen is Leading the SEC," *Fortune* (December, 1966), 163–165, 210–219.

10. Sommer, A. A., Jr., "Conglomerate Disclosure: Friend or Foe?," *The Business Lawyer* (January, 1967), 317–331; reprinted in *The Journal of Accountancy* (May, 1967), 61–67.

11. Rappaport, Louis H., "Problems in Product Line Reporting," *Lybrand Journal*, 48, Nos. 1 & 2 (1967), 3–9.

12. Schachner, Leopold, "Corporate Diversification and Financial Reporting," *The Journal of Accountancy* (April, 1967), 43–50.

13. "SEC Begins Asking Companies to Disclose Contributions Major Lines Make to Profits," *The Wall Street Journal* (April 4, 1967), 3.

14. "Profit Reporting by Divisions?," *Dun's Review* (May, 1967), 29–31, 73–77.

15. *Top Management Looks at Product-Line Reporting*, pamphlet published by the Machinery and Allied Products Institute (1967), 13 pp.

16. "New Disclosures Noted in Annual Reports," *Financial Executive* (June, 1967), 68–73.

17. Mautz, Robert K., "Identification of the Conglomerate Company," *Financial Executive* (July, 1967), 18–26.

18. Nielsen, Oswald, "Canons for Line of Business Reporting," *Management Accounting* (August, 1967), 3–7.

19. Statement of the Accounting Principles Board, September, 1967, "Disclosure of Supplemental Financial Information by Diversified Companies."

20. Mautz, Robert K., "Conglomerate Reporting and Data Reliability," *Financial Executive* (September, 1967), 25–35.

21. ――――, "Bases for a More Detailed Reporting by Diversified Companies," *Financial Executive* (November, 1967), 52–59.

22. Barr, Andrew, "Comments on the Conglomerate Reporting Problem," *Financial Executive* (November, 1967), 39–46.

23. Schwartz, Donald E., "Legal Implications of Product Line Reporting," *The Business Lawyer* (January, 1968), 527–547.

24. Halvorson, Newman T., "Accounting Aspects of Conglomerate Reporting," *The Business Lawyer* (January, 1968), 549–560.

25. Ford, John A., "Reporting Line of Business Profits," *Michigan Business Review* (January, 1968), 20–24.

26. "How Much Data Must Conglomerates Bare?," *Business Week* (January, 20, 1968), 53–56.

27. Mautz, Robert K., "Financial Reporting by Conglomerate Companies," *Financial Executive* (February, 1968), 52–65.